Praise for the
First Edition of
Business Valuation Body of Knowledge

"The beauty of this work is that it points the reader to each professional organization's writings on issues relating to business valuation methodologies and applications. I can't think of an attorney who works with business valuation professionals who should not have this book."

Robert E. Kleeman, Jr., CPA/ABV, ASA, CVA, CFE
Clifton Gunderson, L.L.C.

"*Business Valuation Body of Knowledge* will quickly become one of the foremost authoritative sources on the 'body of knowledge' for business valuations. It is well organized and written in a style which allows it to be used as both a teaching tool and as a reference manual."

R. James Alerding, CPA/ABV, ASA, CVA
Clifton Gunderson, L.L.C.

"When you simply need an answer, Shannon has it for you. The *Body* is a no-nonsense repository of information!"

Stephen J. Bravo, CPA/ABV, CBA, CPF, PFS
Apogee Business Valuations, Inc.

"This book is a 'must have' for every business valuation library.... [Shannon has] done an excellent job of compiling a core body of knowledge that is common to all of the major accredited organizations in the business valuation profession."

Thomas E. Hilton, CPA, CVA
Anders, Minkler & Diehl, LLP

"This book is great. I especially like the cost of capital chapter... It's one of the few books where there is a succinct description of the different methods to determine the cost of capital. I thoroughly enjoyed reading it and it was a great refresher for me."

Mary McCarter, ASA, CFA
Columbia Financial Advisors, Inc.

Business Valuation Body of Knowledge

Workbook

Business Valuation Body of Knowledge

Second Edition

Workbook

Shannon P. Pratt, CFA, FASA, MCBA

with

Alina V. Niculita and Doug Twitchell

JOHN WILEY & SONS, INC.

About the Authors

Dr. Shannon P. Pratt is a founder and managing director of Willamette Management Associates. Founded in 1969, Willamette is one of the oldest and largest independent valuation consulting, economic analysis, and financial advisory services firms, with offices in principal cities across the United States. He is also a member of the board of directors of Paulson Capital Corp., an investment banking firm.

Over the last 35 years, Dr. Pratt has performed valuation engagements for mergers and acquisitions, employee stock ownership plans (ESOPs), fairness opinions, gift and estate taxes, incentive stock options, buy-sell agreements, corporate and partnership dissolutions, dissenting stockholder actions, damages, marital dissolutions, and many other business valuation purposes. He has testified in a wide variety of federal and state courts across the country and frequently participates in arbitration and mediation proceedings.

He holds an undergraduate degree in business administration from the University of Washington and a doctorate in business administration, majoring in finance, from Indiana University. He is a fellow of the American Society of Appraisers, a Master Certified Business Appraiser, a Chartered Financial Analyst, a Certified Business Counselor, and a Certified Mergers and Acquisitions Advisor.

Dr. Pratt's professional recognitions include being designated a life member of the Business Valuation Committee of the American Society of Appraisers, past chairman and a life member of the ESOP Association Advisory Committee on Valuation, a life member of the Institute of Business Appraisers, the recipient of the magna cum laude in business appraisal award from the National Association of Certified Valuation Analysts, and the recipient of the Distinguished Achievement Award from the Portland Society of Financial Analysts. He served two three-year terms (the maximum) as a trustee-at-large of The Appraisal Foundation.

Dr. Pratt is author of *Business Valuation Discounts and Premiums*, *Business Valuation Body of Knowledge*, 2nd edition, *Cost of Capital: Estimation and Applications*, 2nd edition, *Cost of Capital Workbook*, and *The Market Approach to Valuing Businesses* (all published by John Wiley & Sons, Inc.), and *The Lawyer's Business Valuation Handbook* (published by the American Bar Association). He is coauthor of *Valuing a Business: The Analysis and Appraisal of Closely Held Companies*, 4th edition, and *Valuing Small Businesses and Professional Practices*, 3rd edition (both published by McGraw-Hill). He is also coauthor of *Guide to Business Valuations*, 12th edition (published by Practitioners Publishing Company).

He is the editor-in-chief of the monthly newsletter *Shannon Pratt's Business Valuation Update*®. He oversees *BVLibrary.com*ˢᵐ, which includes full texts of court cases, conference presentations and unpublished papers, IRS materials, restricted stock study papers, and pre-IPO study papers and data. He also oversees *Pratt's Stats*™, the official completed transaction database of the International Business Brokers Association, and *BVMarketData.com*ˢᵐ, which includes the online version *of Pratt's Stats*™, as well as *BIZCOMPS*®, *Mergerstat/Shannon Pratt's Control Premium Study*™, *The FMV Restricted Stock Study*™, and the *Valuation Advisors' Lack of Marketability Discount Study*™.

Dr. Pratt develops and teaches business valuation courses for the American Society of Appraisers and the American Institute of Certified Public Accountants, and frequently speaks on business valuation at national legal, professional, and trade association meetings. He also has developed a seminar on business valuation for judges and lawyers.

Alina V. Niculita is the managing editor of *Shannon Pratt's Business Valuation Update®*. She earned her bachelor of economics in banking and finance from the Academy of Economics Studies in Bucharest, Romania, her master's in business administration from CMC Graduate School of Business in the Czech Republic, and her master's in business administration in finance from the Joseph M. Katz Graduate School of Business at the University of Pittsburgh. She is also enrolled in the doctorate of philosophy in systems science/business administration program at Portland State University.

Doug Twitchell is the co-developer of *Pratt's Stats™* and co-manager of *BVMarketData. com*[sm], which contains *Pratt's Stats™*, *Public Stats™*, the *Mergerstat/Shannon Pratt's Control Premium Study™*, *BIZCOMPS®*, *The FMV Restricted Stock Study™*, and *The Valuation Advisors' Lack of Marketability Discount Study™*. He holds a bachelor of science in mechanical and industrial engineering from Clarkson University, a master's in business administration from Portland State University, and an advanced graduate certificate in computational finance from the Oregon Graduate Institute of Science and Technology. Mr. Twitchell has been working at Business Valuation Resources, LLC, since December 1996. Before that, he worked as a mechanical engineer for Fortune 500 companies.

Contents

Preface   xiii
Acknowledgments   xv
Basic Formulas   xvii

Section One: Questions   1

Part I.   Business Valuation Engagement Environment   1

  1. Business Valuation Legal and Regulatory Environment   3
  2. Business Valuation Professional Environment   5
  3. Business Valuation Engagement   8
  4. Litigation Service Engagements   11

Part II.   Terminology and Notation   13

  5. International Glossary of Business Valuation Terms   15
  6. Notation System Used in This Book   17

Part III.   Valuation Approaches and Methods   19

  7. Overview of Valuation Approaches and Methods   21
  8. Income Approach: Cost of Capital   23
  9. Income Approach: Discounting Method   30
 10. Income Approach: Capitalization Method   34
 11. Market Approach: Guideline Public Company Method   38
 12. Market Approach: Guideline Merger and Acquisition Method 41
 13. Prior Transactions, Offers, and Buy-Sell Agreements   45
 14. Adjusted Net Asset Method   47
 15. Excess Earnings Method   49
 16. Discounts and Premiums   51
 17. Reconciliation and Value Conclusion   55

Part IV.   Analysis of the Company   57

18.   **Financial Statement Analysis**   59

19.   **Using Economic and Industry Data**   64

20.   **Site Visits and Interviews**   67

Part V.   Supporting Data   69

21.   **Sources of Supporting Data**   71

Part VI.   Valuations for Specific Purposes   75

22.   **Tax-Related Valuations**   77

23.   **Employee Stock Ownership Plans**   79

24.   **Shareholder Buyouts and Disputes**   82

25.   **Marital Dissolutions**   85

Section Two: Answers   87

Part I.   Business Valuation Engagement Environment   87

1.   **Business Valuation Legal and Regulatory Environment**   89

2.   **Business Valuation Professional Environment**   90

3.   **Business Valuation Engagement**   91

4.   **Litigation Service Engagements**   93

Part II.   Terminology and Notation   95

5.   **International Glossary of Business Valuation Terms**   97

6.   **Notation System Used in This Book**   98

Part III.   Valuation Approaches and Methods   99

7.   **Overview of Valuation Approaches and Methods**   101

8.   **Income Approach: Cost of Capital**   102

9.   **Income Approach: Discounting Method**   105

10.   **Income Approach: Capitalization Method**   108

11.   **Market Approach: Guideline Public Company Method**   111

12.   **Market Approach: Guideline Merger and Acquisition Method**   112

13. Prior Transactions, Offers, and Buy-Sell Agreements   113

14. Adjusted Net Asset Method   114

15. Excess Earnings Method   115

16. Discounts and Premiums   117

17. Reconciliation and Value Conclusion   119

Part IV.   Analysis of the Company   121

18. Financial Statement Analysis   123

19. Using Economic and Industry Data   125

20. Site Visits and Interviews   126

Part V.   Supporting Data   127

21. Sources of Supporting Data   129

Part VI.   Valuations for Specific Purposes   131

22. Tax-related Valuations   133

23. Employee Stock Ownership Plans   134

24. Shareholder Buyouts and Disputes   135

25. Marital Dissolutions   136

CPE Self-Study Examination   137

Index   153

Preface

The *Business Valuation Body of Knowledge Workbook* is designed as a hands-on practical learning experience to supplement the *Business Valuation Body of Knowledge*. It is suitable as a tutorial for beginning appraisers or as a refresher for experienced appraisers. (Even the most experienced professionals will pick up a few things they might have overlooked. Things change rapidly, and this workbook is up-to-date through late 2002.) It is also excellent preparation for those sitting for business valuation credential exams given by the American Institute of Certified Public Accountants (AICPA), American Society of Appraisers (ASA), Institute of Business Appraisers (IBA), National Association of Certified Valuation Analysts (NACVA), Canadian Institute of Chartered Business Valuators (CICBV), or Association for Investment Management and Research (AIMR).

This workbook is also suitable for attorneys, corporate finance officers, or business intermediaries who will be using business appraisals rather than conducting them.

It can be used with either the first or second edition of *Business Valuation Body of Knowledge*, although the workbook tends to put more weight on changes since the first edition. With one exception, the chapter order is the same in both editions and in the workbook. The workbook does not include any questions for Chapter 22, "Sample Case: Shannon's Bull Market."

This workbook covers all the major concepts of the core knowledge related to business appraisal, but it does not include valuation of options or intangible assets.

Like the *Cost of Capital Workbook*, this book is organized in two sections:

1. Section One: Questions
2. Section Two: Answers

The answers section contains not only the answers to the questions, but also some explanation where some discussion beyond the answer would provide useful insight on the subject.

As in the *Cost of Capital Workbook*, four different types of questions (where applicable) are used:

1. Multiple Choice Questions
2. True or False Questions
3. Fill-in-the-Blank Questions
4. Exercises

The exercises include all the basic computational concepts commonly used by business appraisers.

Eight hours of CPE credit are available for those who successfully complete the 40-question self-study examination at the back of the workbook. These hours are *in addition* to the eight hours of CPE credit available for the examination at the back of the *Business Valuation Body of Knowledge* book. (The *Cost of Capital*, 2nd edition, and *Cost of Capital Workbook* are structured the same way, so a total of 32 hours of CPE credit may be earned by completing all four exams.)

I hope that readers will be enriched by this educational opportunity, and I encourage feedback at the e-mail address below.

Shannon Pratt
Portland, Oregon
e-mail: *ShannonP@BVResources.com*

Acknowledgments

The following people reviewed the manuscript, and the workbook reflects their thoughtful consideration and comments:

Nancy Fannon
Baker, Newman & Noyes
Portland, Me.

James S. Rigby
The Financial Valuation Group
Los Angeles, Calif.

Doug Twitchell
Business Valuation Resources, LLC
Portland, Ore.

Alina V. Niculita
Business Valuation Resources, LLC
Portland, Ore.

I would also like to thank Aaron Rotkowski of Willamette Management Associates in Portland, Oregon, who worked through all the questions in the workbook and the CPE examination and gave helpful feedback on the format and content of the workbook.

I especially thank co-authors Alina Niculita and Doug Twitchell for writing chapters 8, 9, 10, and 21, and chapters 18, 19, and 20, respectively. Their contributions are greatly appreciated.

I am very grateful for the continuing support from John Wiley & Sons, especially John DeRemegis, executive editor, Judy Howarth, associate editor, and Louise Jacob, associate managing editor.

Finally, to Tanya Hanson, project manager on this workbook, and Laurie Morrisey, publications department assistant, I would like to express my thanks and appreciation for their outstanding efforts.

Shannon Pratt
Portland, Oregon
November, 2002

Acknowledgments

Basic Formulas

BASIC PRESENT VALUE FORMULA

$$PV = \frac{NCF_1}{(1+k)} + \frac{NCF_2}{(1+k)^2} + \cdots + \frac{NCF_n}{(1+k)^n}$$

where:

PV	= Present value
$NCF_1 \ldots NCF_n$	= Net cash flow (or other measure of economic income) expected in each of the periods 1 through n, n being the final cash flow in the life of the investment
k	= Cost of capital applicable to the defined stream of net cash flow
n	= Number of periods in the series

BASIC CAPITALIZATION FORMULA

$$PV = \frac{NCF_1}{c}$$

where:

PV	= Present value
NCF_1	= Net cash flow expected in the first period immediately following the valuation date
c	= Capitalization rate

FORMULA FOR CONVERTING DISCOUNT RATE TO CAPITALIZATION RATE

$$c = k - g$$

where:

c	= Capitalization rate
k	= Discount rate (cost of capital) for the subject investment
g	= Expected long-term sustainable growth rate in the cash flow available to the subject investment

GORDON GROWTH MODEL

$$PV = \frac{NCF_0(1+g)}{k-g}$$

where:

PV = Present value
NCF_0 = Net cash flow in period 0, the period immediately preceding the valuation date
k = Discount rate (cost of capital)
g = Expected long-term sustainable growth rate in net cash flow to investor

MIDYEAR DISCOUNTING FORMULA

$$PV = \frac{NCF_1}{(1+k)^{0.5}} + \frac{NCF_2}{(1+k)^{1.5}} + \cdots + \frac{NCF_n}{(1+k)^{n-0.5}}$$

where:

PV = Present value
$NCF_1 \ldots NCF_n$ = Net cash flow (or other measure of economic income) expected in each of the periods 1 through n, n being the final cash flow in the life of the investment
k = Cost of capital applicable to the defined stream of net cash flow
n = Number of periods in the series

MIDYEAR CAPITALIZING FORMULA

$$PV = \frac{NCF_1(1+k)^{0.5}}{k-g}$$

where:

PV = Present value
NCF_1 = Net cash flow expected in the first period immediately following the valuation date
k = Discount rate (cost of capital)
g = Expected long-term sustainable growth in net cash flow

MIDYEAR DISCOUNTING FORMULA WITH TERMINAL VALUE

$$PV = \frac{NCF_1}{(1+k)^{0.5}} + \frac{NCF_2}{(1+k)^{1.5}} + \cdots + \frac{NCF_n}{(1+k)^{n-0.5}} + \frac{\dfrac{NCF_n(1+g)(1+k)^{0.5}}{k-g}}{(1+k)^n}$$

where:

PV	= Present value
$NCF_1 \ldots NCF_n$	= Net cash flow expected in each of the periods 1 through n, n being the last period of the discrete cash flow projections
g	= Expected long-term sustainable growth rate in net cash flow, starting with the last period of the discrete projections as the base year
k	= Discount rate (cost of capital)
n	= Number of periods in the series

WEIGHTED AVERAGE COST OF CAPITAL (WACC) FORMULA

$$WACC = (k_e \times W_e) + (k_p \times W_p) + (k_{d(pt)}[1-t] \times W_d)$$

where:

$WACC$	= Weighted average cost of capital
k_e	= Cost of common equity capital
W_e	= Percentage of common equity in the capital structure, at market value
k_p	= Cost of preferred equity
W_p	= Percentage of preferred equity in the capital structure, at market value
$k_{d(pt)}$	= Cost of debt (pretax)
t	= Tax rate
W_d	= Percentage of debt in the capital structure, at market value

FORMULA FOR COST OF EQUITY CAPITAL IN BUILD-UP MODEL

$$E(R_i) = R_f + RP_m + RP_s + RP_u$$

where:

$E(R_i)$	= Expected (market-required) rate of return on security i
R_f	= Rate of return available on a risk-free security as of the valuation date
RP_m	= General equity risk premium for the "market"
RP_s	= Risk premium for small size
RP_u	= Risk premium attributable to the specific company or to the industry (the u stands for unsystematic risk, as defined in Chapter 5)

An additional component may be a factor for industry risk.

FORMULA FOR ARITHMETIC MEAN

$$\bar{X} = \frac{\sum\limits_{1}^{n} R_i}{n}$$

where:

$\bar{X}$ = Mean average

R_i = Return for the ith period (the returns measured for each period are actually excess returns, that is, the difference between the equity market return and the Treasury obligation income return for the period)

n = Number of observation periods

$\sum$ = Sum of (add all the variables that follow)

FORMULA FOR GEOMETRIC MEAN

$$G = \left[\prod_{1}^{n} (1 + R_i) \right]^{\frac{1}{n}} - 1$$

Sometimes also written as:

$$G = \sqrt[n]{\prod_{1}^{n} (1 + R_i)} - 1$$

where:

G = Geometric average

R_i = Return for the ith period (the returns measured for each period are actually excess returns, that is, the difference between the equity market return and the Treasury obligation income return for the period)

n = Number of observation periods

$\prod$ = Product of (multiply together all the variables that follow)

BASIC CAPITAL ASSET PRICING MODEL (CAPM) FORMULA

$$E(R_i) = R_f + B(RP_m)$$

where:

$E(R_i)$ = Expected return (cost of capital) for an individual security

R_f = Rate of return available on a risk-free security (as of the valuation date)

B = Beta

RP_m = Equity risk premium for the market as a whole (or, by definition, the equity risk premium for a security with a beta of 1.0)

EXPANDED CAPM COST OF CAPITAL FORMULA

$$E(R_i) = R_f + B(RP_m) + RP_s + RP_u$$

where:

$E(R_i)$ = Expected rate of return on security i
R_f = Rate of return available on a risk-free security as of the valuation date
B = Beta
RP_m = General equity risk premium for the market
RP_s = Risk premium for small size
RP_u = Risk premium attributable to the specific company (u stands for unsystematic risk)

FORMULA FOR COMPUTING UNLEVERED BETA

This is the formula to go from a levered capital structure beta to the beta that would be assumed for an unlevered capital structure (100% equity).

$$B_u = \frac{B_L}{1 + (1-t)W_d / W_e}$$

where:

B_U = Beta unlevered
B_L = Beta levered
t = Tax rate for the company
W_d = Percent debt in the capital structure
W_e = Percent equity in the capital structure

FORMULA FOR COMPUTING RELEVERED BETA

$$B_L = B_U(1 + (1-t)W_d / W_e)$$

where the definitions of the variables are the same as in the formula for computing unlevered betas

FORMULA FOR ESTIMATING COST OF CAPITAL BY THE SINGLE-STAGE DCF MODEL

$$k = \frac{NCF_0(1+g)}{PV} + g$$

where:

k = Discount rate (cost of capital)
NCF_0 = Net cash flow in period 0, the period immediately preceding the valuation date
g = Expected long-term sustainable growth rate in net cash flow to investor
PV = Present value

FORMULA FOR ESTIMATING COST OF EQUITY CAPITAL BY THE MULTISTAGE DCF MODEL

$$PV = \sum_{n=1}^{5} \frac{[NCF_0(1+g_1)^n]}{(1+k)^n} + \sum_{n=6}^{10} \frac{[NCF_5(1+g_2)^{n-5}]}{(1+k)^n} + \frac{\dfrac{NCF_{10}(1+g_3)}{k-g_3}}{(1+k)^{10}}$$

where:

PV	= Present value
NCF_0	= Net cash flow (or dividend) in the immediately preceding year
$g_1, g_2,$ and g_3	= Expected growth rates in NCF (or dividends) through each of stages 1, 2, and 3, respectively
NCF_5	= Expected net cash flow (or dividend) in the fifth year
NCF_{10}	= Expected net cash flow (or dividend) in the tenth year
k	= Cost of capital (discount rate)

SECTION ONE
Questions

PART I
Business Valuation Engagement Environment

Business Valuation Legal and Regulatory Environment

Before embarking on a business valuation, it is essential to gain an understanding of the legal and regulatory environment. Some aspects of the valuation may be mandated by statutory and/or case law, such as the standard of value; other aspects may be influenced by the law, such as the applicability of certain discounts or premiums.

It is important to understand the purpose of the valuation, that is, the use to which the valuation will be put, because that will determine which laws and regulations govern the valuation. Some valuations are governed by federal law and some by state law, which may vary widely from state to state. Statutes apply for some valuations, but not for others. Binding precedential case law exists for most valuations today but not for all.

Whatever the purpose of the valuation, it is subject to attack, both by regulatory authorities and by parties to the transaction. Knowing and complying with the relevant laws and regulations is essential to avoiding those attacks in the first place and to successfully defending against such attacks should they occur.

MULTIPLE CHOICE QUESTIONS

1. Which of the following is/are governed by federal rather than state law?

    a. Ad valorem (property) taxes

    b. Corporate dissolutions

    c. Dissenting stockholder suits

    d. ESOPs

2. Which of the following Revenue Rulings relates to the excess earnings method?

    a. 59-60

    b. 68-609

    c. 77-287

    d. 83-120

3. Revenue Ruling 93-12 relates to which of the following?

   a. Excess earnings method

   b. Valuation of preferred stock

   c. Discounts for lack of marketability

   d. Family attribution

4. How many judgeships are on the U.S. Tax Court?

   a. 10

   b. 13

   c. 19

   d. 35

TRUE OR FALSE QUESTIONS

5. The Federal Rules of Evidence and the Federal Rules of Civil
   Procedure are both legally binding.   True   False

6 Private Letter Rulings (PLRs) are issued at the taxpayer's request
   regarding how the IRS will treat a proposed transaction.   True   False

7 The *IRS Valuation Training for Appeals Officers Coursebook* may
   not be cited as authority.   True   False

8 Technical Advice Memorandums (TAMs) are released by the IRS
   National Office and arise from questions raised by IRS personnel
   during audits.   True   False

9. Revenue Rulings (RRs) have the force of law.   True   False

10. There can be only one value for a share of stock, regardless of the
    purpose for which it is being valued.   True   False

11. The IRS has published business valuation guidelines.   True   False

FILL-IN-THE-BLANK QUESTION

12. The memorandums that provide nonbinding advice, guidance, and analysis in response to
    questions from IRS agents, attorneys, and appeals officers on both substantive and proce-
    dural issues are called:

    _____ .

Chapter 2

Business Valuation Professional Environment

The Appraisal Foundation was formed in 1986 by a group of professional appraisal organizations involved with real estate, personal property, and business appraisals. Although they do not carry the force of law in most business appraisals, the standards the foundation publishes have come to be widely respected by courts and regulatory authorities.

Four professional organizations in the United States and one in Canada provide certifications and education in business valuation. These organizations all publish their own professional journals, and most have issued standards of their own. Other organizations do not issue certifications in business valuation but have publications and educational programs related to business valuation.

MULTIPLE CHOICE QUESTIONS

1. All of the following are true statements about The Appraisal Foundation EXCEPT:

   a. It appoints members to two independent boards: the Appraisal Standards Board and the Appraisal Qualifications Board.

   b. It is multidisciplinary.

   c. It is supported by members that are individuals.

   d. It has two advisory councils: The Appraisal Foundation Advisory Council (TAFAC), composed of nonprofit organizations and government agencies, and the Industry Advisory Council (IAC), composed of for-profit organizations.

2. Standards issued by The Appraisal Foundation through the Appraisal Standards Board require all of the following for business appraisals EXCEPT:

   a. Disclosure of fee arrangements

   b. Purpose and intended use of the appraisal

   c. Rationale for the valuation methods and procedures considered and employed

   d. Effective date of the appraisal AND date of the report

3. The AICPA issues which of the following credentials?

   a. Accredited in Business Valuation (ABV)

   b. Certified Business Appraiser (CBA)

   c. Certified Valuation Analyst (CVA)

   d. Chartered Business Valuator (CBV)

4. The designation Chartered Financial Analyst is offered by which of the following organizations?

   a. American Society of Appraisers (ASA)

   b. Association for Investment Management and Research (AIMR)

   c. Institute of Business Appraisers (IBA)

   d. Canadian Institute of Chartered Business Valuators (CICBV)

5. Who publishes the *Business Valuation Review*?

   a. American Institute of Certified Public Accountants (AICPA)

   b. Canadian Institute of Chartered Business Valuators (CICBV)

   c. National Association of Certified Valuation Analysts (NACVA)

   d. American Society of Appraisers (ASA)

6. What is the name of the journal published by the Institute of Business Appraisers?

   a. *Business Appraisal Practice*

   b. *The Valuation Examiner*

   c. *Valuation Strategies*

   d. *Financial Analysts Journal*

TRUE OR FALSE QUESTIONS

7. The International Business Brokers Association (IBBA) is oriented primarily to business intermediaries, but membership includes professional advisors such as business appraisers.   True   False

8. The Employee Stock Ownership Plan (ESOP) Association does not issue a professional credential.   True   False

FILL-IN-THE-BLANK QUESTIONS

9. The document issued annually by the Appraisal Standards Board of The Appraisal Foundation is titled:

   _____ .

10. What do the initials CAVS stand for and who sponsors it?

   _____

   _____

Chapter 3

Business Valuation Engagement

When accepting a business valuation assignment, it is essential to understand very clearly what is expected, when it is expected, and what the compensation arrangements are. This should be committed to writing, signed by both the appraiser and the client, and any changes should be memorialized in writing.

MULTIPLE CHOICE QUESTIONS

1. In the context of dissenting stockholder actions, all of the following statements are true EXCEPT:

   a. In most states, the statute defines the valuation date as immediately before the effectuation of the corporate action to which the shareholder objects, excluding any appreciation or depreciation in anticipation of the corporate action, unless exclusion would be inequitable.

   b. In many states, the statute disallows discounts for lack of control and/or lack of marketability.

   c. Delaware tends to emphasize the value of a proportionate share of a going concern and does not allow discounts for minority interest or lack of marketability.

   d. Some states have NO precedential case law interpreting the fair value standard.

2. Which of the following, if any, is the most common statutory standard of value when the purpose of the valuation is property settlement in a marital dissolution?

   a. Fair market value

   b. Fair value

   c. Investment value

   d. None

3. In most states that specify a statutory standard of value for minority oppression actions, what is that standard of value?

    a. Fair market value

    b. Fair value

    c. Investment value

    d. Intrinsic value

4. All of the following are true about *transaction value* (acquisition value) EXCEPT:

    a. It usually is quoted at face value, without adjustment to cash or cash equivalent value.

    b. It usually does *not* impound motivations or circumstances of the specific buyer or seller.

    c. It usually *does* include consideration, if any, paid for noncompete and/or employment agreements.

    d. It may or may not compare with any other definition of value.

5. Which of the following fee arrangements is NOT allowed by the *Uniform Standards of Professional Appraisal Practice (USPAP)*?

    a. Hourly

    b. Fixed fee

    c. Combination of fixed fee and time

    d. Percentage of value

6. A full narrative valuation report typically contains all of the following EXCEPT:

    a. A listing of the data and documents on which the appraiser relied

    b. The professional qualifications of the principal analysts

    c. The dollar amount of the fee or the fee arrangements

    d. A valuation synthesis and conclusion

TRUE OR FALSE QUESTIONS

7. The definition of *fair value* under SFAS 142 (Goodwill and Other Intangible Assets) is the same as or similar to the definition of *fair value* in most state dissenting stockholder statutes.   True   False

8. In many states, the intangible portion of value is excluded by statute for purposes of ad valorem (property) taxation.   True   False

9. Most engagement letters of major firms contain indemnification clauses protecting appraisers in case of lawsuits regarding appraisal.   True   False

10. It is good practice to include the statement of contingent and limiting conditions in both the engagement agreement and the final report.   True   False

11. Valuation engagements usually include investigation for possible fraud.   True   False

12. The engagement letter should state that meeting the prescribed due dates depends on timely receipt of documents and necessary information.   True   False

13. Engagement letters usually state that the valuation is valid only for the use or uses stated in the engagement letter and for the stated effective valuation date.   True   False

FILL-IN-THE-BLANK QUESTIONS

14. The specific value to a *particular* investor or class of investors based on individual investment requirements is called:

    _____ .

15. What is the term used to describe what the value *ought* to be, based on fundamental security analysis, the conclusion of which may or may not coincide with actual market value at any given time?

    _____ .

Chapter 4

Litigation Service Engagements

Career business valuators likely will testify in court or be asked to advise clients regarding alternatives to litigation, so it is helpful to know the rudiments of litigation engagements.

MULTIPLE CHOICE QUESTIONS

1. Under the Federal Rules of Civil Procedure, absent a stipulation or court order, when are experts required to submit written reports?

   a. 120 days before trial, 30 days later for rebuttal evidence

   b. 90 days before trial, 30 days later for rebuttal evidence

   c. 60 days before trial, 30 days later for rebuttal evidence

   d. 30 days before trial, 15 days later for rebuttal evidence

2. Which of the following is a correct statement?

   a. Both arbitration and mediation are binding.

   b. Both arbitration and mediation can be either binding or nonbinding.

   c. Arbitration can be either binding or nonbinding, but mediation is nonbinding.

   d. Neither arbitration nor mediation can be binding.

3. During direct testimony, an expert witness may be asked:

   a. Hypothetical questions but not leading questions

   b. Leading questions but not hypothetical questions

   c. Both hypothetical and leading questions

   d. Neither hypothetical nor leading questions

TRUE OR FALSE QUESTIONS

4. In a *bench trial*, the jury renders the ultimate findings of fact based
    on the evidence the judge determines the jury will use.   True   False

5. Unlike a fact witness, an expert may use the *hearsay exception*,
    which is an opinion based on evidence gained by interviewing others,
    but the information gained must be the type on which experts in the
    field normally rely.   True   False

6. Lawyers can issue subpoenas either to testify or to produce
    documents, but subpoenas are more easily quashed (challenged) than
    summonses, which are issued by judges to order an individual to
    appear in court.   True   False

7. Like the federal court system, most states have three levels: trial courts,
    courts of appeals, and state supreme courts.   True   False

8. The U.S. Tax Court exists only to resolve disputes between the
    Internal Revenue Service and taxpayers.   True   False

FILL-IN-THE-BLANK QUESTIONS

9. Rule 702, "Testimony by an Expert," and Rule 703, "Bases of Opinion Testimony by
    Experts," are examples of which body of binding rules?

    _____ .

10. What is the term used to allow an opposing attorney to question a witness about his or her
    qualifications after the expert's qualifications have been presented to the court but before
    the court has decided to qualify the witness as an expert?

    _____ .

PART II
Terminology and Notation

International Glossary of Business Valuation Terms

The language of finance has so many ambiguities that it is difficult enough to get one professional business valuation group to agree on definitions of terms, let alone five. This glossary, however, has been officially approved by the following five organizations:

1. American Institute of Certified Public Accountants
2. American Society of Appraisers
3. Canadian Institute of Chartered Business Valuators
4. Institute of Business Appraisers
5. National Association of Certified Valuation Analysts

MULTIPLE CHOICE QUESTIONS

1. Which of the following is a multivariate model for estimating the cost of equity capital, which incorporates several systematic risk factors?

    a. Build-up model

    b. Capital Asset Pricing Model (CAPM)

    c. Discounted cash flow model

    d. Arbitrage pricing model

2. In the lexicon of valuation, the act, manner, and technique of performing the steps of an appraisal method is called what?

    a. Standard of value

    b. Premise of value

    c. Valuation approach

    d. Valuation procedure

3. A measure of the systematic risk of a stock is called what?

   a. Beta

   b. Business risk

   c. Financial risk

   d. Investment risk

4. What is the value to a particular investor based on individual investment requirements and expectations?

   a. Fair market value

   b. Fair value

   c. Investment value

   d. Intrinsic value

TRUE OR FALSE QUESTIONS

5. The current cost of an identical new property is called *replacement cost*.   True   False

6. A multiple is the inverse of a capitalization rate.   True   False

7. Strictly speaking, *goodwill* is that intangible asset arising as a result of the name, reputation, customer loyalty, location, products, and similar factors not separately identified.   True   False

8. A *fairness opinion* is an opinion about whether the consideration for a transaction is fair from a financial point of view.   True   False

FILL-IN-THE-BLANK QUESTIONS

9. Financial statements in which each line is expressed as a percentage of the total are called:

   _____ .

10. A discount rate at which the present value of the future cash flows of the investment equals the cost of the investment is called the:

    _____ .

Chapter 6

Notation System Used in This Book

The notation system used in this book is becoming widely accepted as the standard notation in the profession, thus eliminating a great deal of confusion. It was first introduced in the third edition of *Valuing a Business* by Shannon Pratt, Robert Reilly, and Robert Schweihs, and then continued in the fourth edition and all of the other books by Pratt and coauthors. *Valuing a Business* has been adopted as the basic official text of the American Society of Appraisers' courses BV201 through BV204 and by the Internal Revenue Service for its in-house business valuation training course.

Use of this notation system in appraisal reports will further enhance the trend toward uniformity in the profession.

MULTIPLE CHOICE QUESTIONS

1. $\overline{X}$ is the symbol for what type of average?

   a. Mean

   b. Median

   c. Mode

   d. Harmonic mean

2. In the formula for computing the equity risk premium, RP_m usually stands for the difference in returns between the risk-free rate and what?

   a. Standard & Poor's 500 Index (S&P 500)

   b. New York Stock Exchange (NYSE) and American Stock Exchange (AMEX)

   c. NYSE, AMEX, and Nasdaq Stock Market (NASDAQ)

   d. NYSE, AMEX, NASDAQ, and all other over-the-counter (OTC) stocks

3. The subscript $_0$ usually refers to what period or periods?

    a. The average of some number of periods preceding the valuation date

    b. The base period, usually the latest year immediately preceding the valuation date

    c. The estimate for the period (usually a year) immediately following the valuation date

    d. The average of estimates for some number of periods following the valuation date

4. In the system of notation usually used for business valuation, a lower-case t (usually italicized) stands for:

    a. Terminal value

    b. Time (expressed in number of periods, usually years)

    c. Tax rate

    d. Total

TRUE OR FALSE QUESTIONS

5. In the formula for computing a weighted average cost of capital (WACC), it is assumed that the weights are at book value.   True   False

6. The lower case letter k (usually italicized) stands for capitalization rate.   True   False

FILL-IN-THE-BLANK QUESTIONS

7. What do the letters EBITDA stand for?

    _____ .

8. What do the letters MVIC stand for?

    _____ .

PART III
Valuation Approaches and Methods

Chapter 7

Overview of Valuation Approaches and Methods

This chapter presents a broad overview of the methodology of business valuation, including the strengths and weaknesses of the various methods and how the purpose of the valuation affects the choice of methodology.

MULTIPLE CHOICE QUESTIONS

1. Which of the following is a correct statement?

   a. The statutory standard of value for virtually all tax-related valuations, including ESOPs, is *fair market value*.

   b. The statutory standard of value for virtually all tax-related valuations, except ESOPs, is *fair market value*.

   c. The statutory standard of value for tax-related valuations varies, depending on the nature of the tax.

   d. There is no statutory standard of value for tax-related valuations; the analyst must look to the case law.

2. Which of the following is a correct statement with respect to dissenting stockholder actions?

   a. The statutory standard of value in most states is *fair market value*, interpreted consistently from state to state.

   b. The statutory standard of value in most states is *fair market value*, but the analyst must look at state case law for interpretation.

   c. The statutory standard of value in most states is *fair value*, interpreted consistently from state to state.

   d. The statutory standard of value in most states is *fair value*, but the analyst must look at state case law for interpretation.

3. All of the following statements regarding valuations for marital dissolutions are true EXCEPT:

   a. Most family law courts have broad discretion to choose among valuation methods on a case-by-case basis.

   b. The discounted cash flow method is gradually becoming more accepted in family law courts.

   c. Statutory standards of value for marital dissolutions vary widely from state to state.

   d. The excess earnings method is widely used in family law courts.

TRUE OR FALSE QUESTIONS

4. There are more total transactions available for the guideline merger and acquisition method than for the guideline public company method.　　True　　False

5. The excess earnings method, the asset accumulation method, and the guideline merger and acquisition method all tend to result in control values, while the discounted cash flow method may produce either a control value or a minority value depending on the cash flows used in the projections.　　True　　False

6. If the standard of *fair market value* appears in a court opinion in a marital dissolution case, the analyst should adhere to the procedures for fair market value for any case in that jurisdiction.　　True　　False

7. The Internal Revenue Service position on the excess earnings method (articulated in Revenue Ruling 68-609) is that it should be used "only if no better method is available."　　True　　False

FILL-IN-THE-BLANK QUESTIONS

8. What are the three basic approaches to valuation?

   _____

   _____

   _____

9. In the context of the traditional three-tiered hierarchy, the broadest category is approaches; within approaches there are _____ , and within these there are _____ .

10. Regardless of the approach or methods used, appraisers can value just the equity, or the value of all the equity and long-term debt, known as _____ .

Chapter 8

Income Approach: Cost of Capital

Cost of capital is a central topic in business valuation and one of the most difficult pieces of the puzzle to estimate. This chapter discusses a few methods available for the practitioner to estimate the cost of equity, debt, and preferred equity for a private or public company.

While working through this chapter, become familiar with the main methods of estimating the cost of equity; the composition and calculation of the weighted average cost of capital (WACC); and applying the single- and multistage discounted cash flow (DCF) models.

MULTIPLE CHOICE QUESTIONS

1. The cost of capital can be defined as all of the following EXCEPT:

   a. Cost of capital is the expected rate of return that a company can pay its investors.

   b. In economic terms, cost of capital is an opportunity cost.

   c. Cost of capital is market driven.

   d. Cost of capital is based on the principle of substitution.

2. Which of the following components in a company's capital structure has (have) a cost of capital?

   a. Common equity

   b. Common equity and preferred equity

   c. Common equity and debt

   d. Common equity, preferred equity, and debt

3. What are the basic components of cost of capital?

   a. A real rate of return and risk

   b. A nominal rate of return, expected inflation, and risk

   c. A real rate of return, expected inflation, and risk

   d. A risk-free rate, expected inflation, and risk

4. The concept of the "time value of money" refers to the combination of which of the following two items?

   a. A risk-free rate and risk

   b. Risk and expected inflation

   c. A nominal rate of return and expected inflation

   d. A "real" rate of return and expected inflation

5. If Company ABC values a potential acquisition target XYZ by discounting expected cash flows for XYZ using its own (ABC's) cost of capital, what will the resulting value be?

   a. Fair market value

   b. Investment value

   c. Fair value

   d. Intrinsic value

6. When estimating the fair market value of a subsidiary, which cost of capital should be used to discount its future cash flows?

   a. The parent's cost of capital

   b. The subsidiary's cost of capital

   c. A blended discount rate for both the parent and the subsidiary

   d. The cost of capital of the company that will potentially acquire the subsidiary

7. Which of the following is true about cost of capital?

   a. It is a function of the investor.

   b. It is usually stated in nominal terms.

   c. It is usually based on expected returns relative to book prices.

   d. It is based on actual past returns on comparable investments.

8. When estimating cost of capital in a country with hyperinflation, one method is to state:

   a. Both returns and cost of capital in nominal terms

   b. Expected returns in nominal terms and cost of capital in real terms

   c. Expected returns in real terms and cost of capital in nominal terms

   d. Both expected returns and cost of capital in real terms

9. Which of the following is the correct relationship between the pretax cost of debt ($K_{d(pt)}$), the after-tax cost of debt (K_d), and the tax rate (t)?

    a. $K_{d(pt)} = K_d \times (1 - t)$

    b. $K_d = K_{d(pt)} \times (1 - t)$

    c. $K_{d(pt)} = K_d \times t$

    d. $K_d = K_{d(pt)} \times t$

10. All of the following are hidden costs to consider when estimating cost of debt EXCEPT:

    a. Points up front

    b. Non–tax-deductible interest on debt

    c. Compensating bank balance requirements

    d. Personal guarantees

11. Which of the following rates (is) are directly observable in the market?

    a. Cost of equity and cost of preferred equity

    b. Cost of debt and cost of equity

    c. Cost of debt and cost of preferred equity

    d. Cost of preferred equity only

12. The WACC is a blended rate of which of the following rates?

    a. Cost of common equity capital and cost of debt

    b. Cost of preferred equity capital and cost of debt

    c. Cost of common equity capital and preferred equity capital

    d. Cost of common equity capital, cost of preferred equity capital, and cost of debt

13. In the WACC formula, which of the following is multiplied by $(1 - t)$?

    a. Pretax cost of common equity

    b. Pretax cost of preferred equity

    c. Pretax cost of debt

    d. After-tax cost of debt

14. Assume that the pretax cost of debt for a company is 10% and that it has a 30% tax rate. The after-tax cost of debt equals:

    a. 10%

    b. 7%

    c. 3%

    d. 1%

15. A "risk-free rate" includes all of the following risks EXCEPT:

    a. Maturity risk

    b. Default risk

    c. Horizon risk

    d. Interest rate risk

16. The equity risk premium for a specific company may include any of the following elements EXCEPT:

    a. Interest rate risk premium

    b. General equity risk premium

    c. Investment-specific equity risk premium

    d. Size premium

17. The Capital Asset Pricing Model (CAPM) estimates the cost of equity capital as:

    a. A risk-free rate plus a general equity risk premium

    b. A risk-free rate times a general risk premium

    c. A risk-free rate plus a linear function of a measure of systematic risk times the general equity risk premium

    d. A risk-free rate plus a linear function of a measure of systematic risk times the specific equity risk premium

18. The component(s) that is (are) added to the modified (expanded) CAPM, compared with the simple CAPM, is (are):

    a. Risk premium for small stock size

    b. Specific equity risk premium

    c. Risk premium for small stock size and maturity risk

    d. Risk premium for small stock size and unsystematic risk

19. All of the following are choices that analysts must make when estimating cost of equity capital EXCEPT:

    a. Short-term, intermediate-term, or long-term risk-free rate

    b. Short-term, intermediate-term, or long-term equity risk premium

    c. Short-term, intermediate-term, or long-term beta

    d. Arithmetic average or geometric average equity risk premium

20. Which of the following is the correct relationship between levered and unlevered beta (B_L and B_U)?

    a. $\dfrac{B_U}{B_L} = 1 + (1 - t)\,(W_d/W_e)$

    b. $B_L = \dfrac{B_U}{1 + (1 - t)\,(W_d/W_e)}$

    c. $B_U = B_L[1 + (1 - t)\,(W_d/W_e)]$

    d. $B_L = B_U[1 + (1 - t)\,(W_d/W_e)]$

TRUE OR FALSE QUESTIONS

21. Since risk cannot be observed directly, analysts usually look at historical data to estimate it.   True   False

22. In the context of business valuation, the cost of capital equals the discount rate, which in turn equals the total expected rate of return.   True   False

23. If a minority interest is subject to valuation, then a hypothetical capital structure usually is employed.   True   False

24. The risk-free rate is one of the components of the general equity risk premium.   True   False

25. In CAPM, the size premium is multiplied by beta.   True   False

26. Betas for private companies are directly observable in the market.   True   False

27. The arbitrage pricing model is still widely used today, especially for
    very small companies.   True   False

FILL-IN-THE-BLANK QUESTIONS

28. The principle of _____ refers to the concept that an
    investor will not invest in a particular asset if a more attractive substitute exists.

29. _____ is the degree of uncertainty that all investors will
    realize the expected returns at the specified times.

30. The blended average of the costs of the capital structure components is the company's
    _____ .

31. Cost of equity covers a wide band of required returns because of the wide range of
    _____ .

32. _____ is a measure of systematic risk.

33. All Ibbotson Associates' return data are _____ entity-level
    income taxes and _____ personal-level income taxes.

EXERCISES

The following are known about Company XYZ:

	Common Equity	Preferred Equity	Debt
Book Value	$1,000,000	$500,000	$500,000
Market Value	$2,000,000	$1,000,000	$500,000

Cost of debt pretax	10%
Tax rate	40%
Cost of common equity	20%
Cost of preferred equity	15%

34. Compute the after-tax cost of debt for Company XYZ.

35. Compute the WACC for Company XYZ.

The following are known:

Risk-free rate	6.25%
Beta for Company XYZ	0.75
General equity risk premium	5.5%

36. Compute the cost of equity for Company XYZ.

Given the following:

Unlevered beta	0.80
Tax rate	40%
Capital structure:	60% equity; 40% debt

37. Compute the levered beta.

Given the following:

Levered beta	1.25
Tax rate	40%
Capital structure:	60% equity; 40% debt

38. Compute the unlevered beta.

Given the following:

$NCF_0 = \$1,000,000$
$g = 10\%$
$k = 20\%$

39. Compute the value of Company ABC using the single-stage DCF model.

Chapter 9

Income Approach: Discounting Method

Understanding the theory and applications of the discounted economic income model is at the heart of the modern financial and economic theory. The model is used not only for valuing businesses but for any type of asset whose future benefits and risk can be estimated or approximated using market data. While reading and working through this chapter, pay special attention to the mechanics of the present value formula, the concept of terminal value and methods of estimating, and to applying the midyear and year-end conventions.

MULTIPLE CHOICE QUESTIONS

1. All of the following are true about the discounted economic income method to valuation EXCEPT:

   a. It is the most objective method with very few elements that depend exclusively on the analyst's judgment and experience.

   b. It is based on the premise that a financial investment is worth the sum of all the future benefits discounted to the present.

   c. According to economic theory, it is the proper way to value any investment.

   d. It involves the use of cost of capital in the form of a discount rate.

2. All of the following are accepted methods of estimating terminal value EXCEPT:

   a. Liquidation or salvage method

   b. Market multiple method

   c. Capitalization method

   d. Discounting method

3. All of the following statements about the relationship between the midyear and year-end conventions are false EXCEPT:

   a. The midyear convention always results in a lower present value than the year-end convention.

   b. The midyear convention always results in a higher present value than the year-end convention.

   c. The midyear convention results in the same present value as the year-end convention if the cash flows are equal.

   d. One cannot make a generalization about the relationship between the midyear and year-end conventions.

4. "Terminal value" of an investment refers to:

   a. The expected cash flow in the last year of the discrete projection period (n)

   b. The expected cash flow in the year after the last year of the discrete projection period ($n + 1$)

   c. The present value of the expected cash flows beyond the discrete projection period

   d. The last cash flow that the investment yields with no regard to its timing

TRUE OR FALSE QUESTIONS

5. Net cash flow is the only measure of economic income that can be used with the discounted economic income method.   True   False

6. When applying the discounted economic income method, analysts must match the measure of economic income to the discount rate used in the model.   True   False

7. Net cash flow is likely to be higher than net income for a growing company.   True   False

8. The terminal value must be discounted to present value by the number of years of the discrete projection period plus 1 ($n + 1$).   True   False

9. Whether the discounted economic income method produces a minority or a control value depends primarily on the choice of discount rate (cost of capital).   True   False

10. Discounts for lack of marketability for controlling interests are usually much less than those for minority interests.   True   False

FILL-IN-THE-BLANK QUESTIONS

11. The discounted economic income method can be used for valuing either
    _____ or _____ .

12. When using the discounting method for cost of equity, the discount rate should be
    _____ ; when using it for invested capital, the discount rate
    should be _____ .

EXERCISES

The following are known about Company ABC:

Net income (after taxes)	$1,000,000
Noncash charges (previously subtracted to arrive at net income)	$ 200,000
Capital expenditures	$ 300,000
Additions to net working capital	$ 100,000
New debt incurred	$ 200,000
Debt repayments	$ 100,000
Interest expense paid (net of tax deduction)	$ 50,000

13. Compute net cash flow to equity.

14. Compute net cash flow to invested capital.

The following are known about a specific investment:

- The cash flows at the end of years 1, 2, and 3 are $100, $100, and $1,100, respectively.
- The market yield on comparable investments is 10%.

15. Compute the value of the investment as of now. Would you buy this series of cash flows
    for $950 today?

16. The following probability distribution is known about cash flow in period 1. Compute the expected value of cash flow in period 1. Is this a symmetrical or skewed distribution?

Amount	Probability of Occurrence
$1,000	10%
$1,100	15%
$1,200	45%
$1,300	15%
$1,400	15%

17. Given that a specific investment will yield $100, $100, and $1,100 in years 1, 2, and 3, respectively, and 10% is the yield on comparable investments, compute the value of the investment as of now, using the midyear convention. How would this value compare with the value of the investment if the year-end convention were used? Would you buy this series of cash flows for $950 today?

Chapter 10

Income Approach: Capitalization Method

Capitalization and discounting are different methods within the income approach to valuation. When working through this chapter, pay special attention to differences between the capitalization rate and the discount rate, to the Gordon Growth Model, and to the computation of present value under the midyear and year-end conventions. Also, be able to distinguish between sets of circumstances that may indicate which method would be the most appropriate in a given scenario.

MULTIPLE CHOICE QUESTIONS

1. Which of the following is (are) true about the capitalization method?

   I.   In the capitalization method, each year's projected economic return is discounted by a different time factor.

   II. In the capitalization method, a base amount is assumed to be constant or to increase or decrease at some predictable average rate in perpetuity.

   III. In the capitalization method, all changes in expected future returns are captured in the denominator, not in the numerator.

   IV. The discounting method is a shorter version of the capitalization method.

      a. I, II

      b. II, III

      c. III, IV

      d. II

2. The capitalization rate equals:

   a. The growth rate minus the discount rate

   b. The discount rate minus the growth rate

   c. The growth rate plus the discount rate

   d. The discount rate plus the growth rate

3. The capitalization method produces the same value as the discounting method if:

   a. The capitalization rate equals the discount rate

   b. The sum of cash flows used with the discounting method equals the cash flows used in the capitalization method

   c. The growth rate is estimated accurately

   d. The discount rate equals the capitalization rate plus the growth rate

4. The Gordon Growth Model is:

   a. A formula for a discounting model

   b. A formula for accurately estimating growth rates for investments

   c. A formula for reflecting variable growth in the capitalization method

   d. A formula for reflecting constant growth in the capitalization method

5. In the two-stage model, the terminal or residual value must be discounted for which number of periods?

   a. $n - 1$

   b. n

   c. $n + 1$

   d. $n + 2$

TRUE OR FALSE QUESTIONS

6. The major difference between discounting and capitalizing is how the analyst reflects changes over time in future cash flows.   True   False

7. The capitalization method can be applied only to estimate the equity value.   True   False

8. The capitalization method cannot be applied if the growth rate is negative.   True   False

9. The capitalization method allows for a "no-growth" and a "growth" methodology.   True   False

FILL-IN-THE-BLANK QUESTIONS

10. In the capitalization method, some base amount of return is divided by a rate called a
_____ rate.

11. _____ is the preferred measure of economic income to use
in the capitalization method.

12. The Gordon Growth Model is used in the two-stage discounting method to estimate the
_____ .

EXERCISES

The following are given about a stock:

- A preferred stock pays $4 per share per year.
- The market yield for comparable investments is 8%.
- The preferred stock is assumed to be issued in perpetuity with no prospect of liquidation.

13. Compute the estimated fair market value for the stock.

The following are known about Company ABC:

- Net cash flow (NCF) in the previous period was $200.
- Cost of capital (k) is 15%.
- Sustainable rate of growth in perpetuity is expected to be 5%.

14. Compute the estimated fair market value for Company ABC.

The following are known about a particular investment opportunity X:

- Expected net cash flows at the end of the years 1, 2, and 3, are $150, $250, and $350, respectively.
- Beyond year 3, cash flow is expected to increase at a steady rate of 5% in perpetuity.
- The cost of capital for this investment is estimated to be 10%.

15. Estimate the fair market value of this investment at the beginning of the year using the year-end convention. Would you invest for a price of $6,000?

16. Estimate the terminal or residual value at the beginning of year 4.

17. Compute the present value of the terminal (residual) value as of the beginning of year 1.

18. Estimate the fair market value of this investment at the beginning of year 1 using the midyear convention. Would you invest for a price of $6,000?

The following are known about a particular investment opportunity Z:

- Net cash flow in period 0 was $1,000.
- Cost of capital (discount rate) is 15%.
- Sustainable rate of growth in net cash flow from year 0 to perpetuity is expected to be 5%.

19. Estimate the fair market value of this investment assuming cash flows are received at the end of the year. Would you invest for $10,000?

20. Estimate the fair market value of this investment assuming cash flows are received more or less evenly throughout the year. Would you buy this investment for $10,000?

Chapter 11

Market Approach: Guideline Public Company Method

The idea of the guideline public company method is to observe the prices at which public stocks trade and to relate those prices to fundamental financial variables of those companies, such as earnings and book values. Such ratios (e.g., price/earnings ratio) are what we call "valuation multiples." We can apply those valuation multiples to the fundamental financial variables for our subject company to derive indications of value.

MULTIPLE CHOICE QUESTIONS

1. All of the following are valid invested capital multiples EXCEPT:

   a. MVIC/sales

   b. MVIC/net income

   c. MVIC/EBIT

   d. MVIC/EBITDA

2. All of the following time periods are valid for earnings in the guideline public company method EXCEPT:

   a. Five years average historical earnings

   b. Immediate past 12 month's earnings

   c. One year ahead projected earnings

   d. Five years ahead average projected earnings

3. Which of the following is the best statement regarding adjustments to guideline public financial statements?

   a. They should be adjusted to eliminate extraordinary and/or nonrecurring items.

   b. If guideline and subject company financial statements are on different inventory accounting bases, adjust both to FIFO (first in, first out).

   c. Both a and b.

   d. The analyst should not make adjustments to guideline public company financial statements.

4. All of the following are correct statements regarding the selection and weighting of valuation multiples EXCEPT:

   a. Lean toward equity multiples when valuing controlling interests.

   b. Invested capital multiples may be used for minority interests, especially if capital structures among the companies are quite different.

   c. Usually put most weight on multiples with the lowest coefficient of variation.

   d. The analyst may use either mathematical or subjective weightings of the selected multiples.

5. Which of the following levels of value generally is indicated by the guideline public company method?

   a. Acquisition value

   b. Control value

   c. Marketable minority value

   d. Nonmarketable minority value

TRUE OR FALSE QUESTIONS

6. Revenue Ruling 59-60 advocates the guideline public company method.   True   False

7. Corporations can register with the SEC for a public offering, but partnerships cannot.   True   False

8. All companies required to file annual reports with the SEC must file electronically, so access through EDGAR is free on the Internet.   True   False

9. The SEC requires public companies to make disclosures beyond those required in audited statements of nonpublic companies.   True   False

10. EDGAR is searchable by SIC code.   True   False

FILL-IN-THE-BLANK QUESTIONS

11. What do the initials EDGAR stand for?

_____ .

12. What is a 10-K?

_____ .

13. What is a 10-Q?

_____ .

14. What is the number of the report required to be filed with the SEC when a public company has significant special events?

_____ .

15. What do the initials SIC stand for?

_____ .

Chapter 12

Market Approach: Guideline Merger and Acquisition Method

The guideline merger and acquisition method differs from the guideline public company method in that the observed transactions involve entire companies or controlling interests in companies rather than day-to-day transactions of minority interests. They may include companies that were either public or private prior to the control transaction.

There are a finite number of public companies that sell each year—about 700 on average, although the level of this activity varies greatly from year to year. By contrast, thousands of private companies change hands each year.

One difference between the guideline merger and acquisition method and the guideline public company method is the proximity in time between the guideline transaction and the effective valuation date. In the guideline public company method, it is possible to observe transactions either on the effective date or very close to it. Mergers and acquisitions, on the other hand, occur on dates removed from the effective valuation date, so it is sometimes necessary to adjust for the time difference. These adjustments may be in the form of internal company data and/or changes in the industry.

MULTIPLE CHOICE QUESTIONS

1. Which of the following databases contains transaction multiples only for acquired *public* companies?

   a. *Pratt's Stats*™

   b. *Mergerstat/Shannon Pratt's Control Premium Study*™

   c. *BIZCOMPS*®

   d. *Done Deals*®

2. In the *Mergerstat/Shannon Pratt's Control Premium Study*™, control premiums are shown relative to which of the following prior prices?

   a. One day, two days, one week, one month, and the Mergerstat unaffected price

   b. One day, one week, two weeks, one month, and the Mergerstat unaffected price

   c. One day, one week, one month, two months, and the Mergerstat unaffected price

   d. One day, one week, one month, three months, and the Mergerstat unaffected price

3. If using guideline merger and acquisition transactions to value a minority interest by the standard of fair market value, which of the following discounts, if any, usually would be appropriate?

   a. Neither minority nor marketability

   b. Minority but not marketability

   c. Marketability but not minority

   d. Both minority and marketability

4. Which of the following databases contains a mixture of companies that were public and companies that were private prior to the transaction?

   a. *Mergerstat/Shannon Pratt's Control Premium Study*™

   b. *Done Deals*®

   c. *BIZCOMPS*®

   d. *IBA Market Database*

5. How many valuation multiples are included for each transaction in the *IBA Market Database*?

   a. 2

   b. 5

   c. 8

   d. 10

6. How many valuation multiples are included for each transaction in the *BIZCOMPS*® database?

   a. 2

   b. 5

   c. 8

   d. 10

7. How many valuation multiples are included for each transaction in the *Pratt's Stats™* database?

    a. 2

    b. 5

    c. 8

    d. 10

8. How many valuation multiples are included for each transaction in the *Mergerstat/Shannon Pratt's Control Premium Study™* database?

    a. 2

    b. 5

    c. 8

    d. 10

9. Assuming the acquirer has no previous ownership interest in the target company, what percentage of the stock of a company must be acquired for the transaction to be selected for inclusion in the *Mergerstat/Shannon Pratt's Control Premium Study™* database?

    a. 30%

    b. 50.1%

    c. 66⅔%

    d. 80%

TRUE OR FALSE QUESTIONS

10. The proliferation of data on merged and acquired companies in recent years has made the merger and acquisition method much more feasible and widely used.   True   False

11. Almost all of the transactions in the various online merger and acquisition databases occurred at arm's length.   True   False

12. The guideline merger and acquisition method is similar to the guideline publicly traded company method, but it deals with transfers of control interests rather than minority interests.   True   False

FILL-IN-THE-BLANK QUESTIONS

13. Of the private company transaction databases, which has the largest number of transactions?

   _____ .

14. Of the private company transaction databases, which has the most data per transaction?

   _____ .

Chapter 13

Prior Transactions, Offers, and Buy-Sell Agreements

Prior transactions (a sale of either the entire company or minority interests) can provide a source of the best evidence of value. Since they represent transfers of ownership, they are classified under the market approach. The same market multiples used in the guideline public company and guideline transaction methods can be derived from past transactions and applied to the company's data as of the effective valuation date.

TRUE OR FALSE QUESTIONS

1. If prior transactions were not on an arm's-length basis, they may provide weak (or no) evidence of value.   True   False

2. In researching prior transactions, acquisitions made by the company should be considered.   True   False

3. A buy-sell agreement that is legally enforceable is determinative of value for estate tax purposes.   True   False

FILL-IN-THE-BLANK QUESTIONS

4. Since prior transactions, by definition, are at points in time different from the effective date of the current transaction, what two types of adjustments might be needed to account for the difference in time?

_____

_____

5. What four questions should the analyst investigate regarding prior offers for the company or an interest in it?

_____

_____

_____

_____

6. What five questions should an analyst investigate when evaluating the effect of a buy-sell agreement on a stock's value?

_____

_____

_____

_____

_____

Chapter 14

Adjusted Net Asset Method

The adjusted net asset method (also called the asset accumulation method) adjusts all the assets and liabilities to fair market value. The difference between the value of the assets and the value of the liabilities represents the value of the company. In the broadest application of the method, both tangible and intangible assets and liabilities would be included, whether or not they appeared on the balance sheet.

MULTIPLE CHOICE QUESTIONS

1. All of the following are situations suggesting an asset appraisal by a qualified party EXCEPT:

   a. Asset liquidations are a consideration.

   b. Purchase price allocations are required.

   c. Nonoperating assets are a factor.

   d. A manufacturing company is highly profitable; however, its equipment is well maintained but old and is heavily depreciated on the books.

2. Which approach is used most often in valuing intangible assets?

   a. Income approach

   b. Market approach

   c. Cost approach

   d. Rules of thumb

3. Which of the following issues certifications in both real estate and machinery and equipment appraisal?

   a. American Society of Appraisers

   b. Appraisal Institute

   c. National Association of Certified Valuation Analysts

   d. The Appraisal Foundation

4. What is usually the primary type of inventory for service firms?

   a. Raw materials

   b. Work in process

   c. Finished goods

   d. Inventory held for sale

TRUE OR FALSE QUESTIONS

5. The term *real estate* is a subset of the broader term *real property*,
   with *real estate* representing the tangible elements of real property,
   such as land and buildings.   True   False

6. The asset approach generally indicates a control value. So, if valuing
   a minority stock interest starting with the asset approach, the indicated
   value usually must be discounted for *both* minority status and lack of
   marketability.   True   False

7. Since 1998, the U.S. Tax Court sometimes has recognized a discount
   for a C corporation holding highly appreciated stock and at other
   times has rejected such a discount.   True   False

8. The *Uniform Standards of Professional Appraisal Practice (USPAP)*
   apply to appraisals of all kinds of assets.   True   False

FILL-IN-THE-BLANK QUESTIONS

9. When adjusting asset values on the balance sheet, what are the two primary premises of
   value?

   _____

   _____

10. The real estate appraisal method that is analogous to the business valuation discounting
    method is called the _____ . The real estate appraisal
    method that is most analogous to the business valuation capitalization method is called the
    _____ .

Chapter 15

Excess Earnings Method

Possibly because it has been around so long and seems simple on its surface, the excess earnings method is widely used and also misused. Its apparent simplicity can be deceiving; the method is full of ambiguities and opportunities to go wrong.

MULTIPLE CHOICE QUESTIONS

1. In what year was the excess earnings method first promulgated?

    a. 1920

    b. 1934

    c. 1948

    d. 1968

2. Which Revenue Ruling addresses the excess earnings method?

    a. 59-60

    b. 68-609

    c. 77-287

    d. 83-120

3. In what legal context is the excess earnings method most widely used?

    a. Gift, estate, and income taxes

    b. Marital dissolutions

    c. Shareholder disputes such as dissenting stockholders and minority oppressions

    d. Adjudication of reasonable compensation disputes

TRUE OR FALSE QUESTIONS

4. There is virtually unanimous agreement that the value estimated by
   the excess earnings method is control value.   True   False

5. When the excess earnings method is used, its implementation is highly
   consistent.   True   False

6. The Revenue Ruling on the excess earnings method states that the
   return on tangible assets should be 8 to 10% and the capitalization
   rate on excess earnings should be 15 to 20%.   True   False

7. The excess earnings ("formula" approach) Revenue Ruling states
   that the "earnings to which the formula is applied should fairly reflect
   the probable future earnings."   True   False

8. In a partnership or sole proprietorship, the "earnings" referred to in
   the IRS Revenue Ruling include the compensation to the partners or
   proprietor.   True   False

9. The IRS encourages the use of the excess earnings method for the
   valuation of intangible assets.   True   False

EXERCISES

The following are known about Company ABC:

Net tangible asset value	$100,000
Normalized annual economic income	$40,000
Required rate of return to support tangible assets	8%
Capitalization rate for excess earnings	16%

10. Value Company ABC by the excess earnings method.

11. What would be the indicated weighted averaged cost of capital (WACC) capitalization rate
    for Company ABC?

12. Assuming that this is a small service business, is the value calculated by using the excess
    earnings method with the given assumptions a reasonable value? Why or why not?

Chapter 16

Discounts and Premiums

Often there is more money involved in the issues of discounts and premiums than in the issues leading up to the base value to which the discounts or premiums will be applied. Vast amounts of data exist to help quantify discounts for lack of marketability, which is fortunate, because the discount for lack of marketability is the largest and most frequent of the money disputes over discounts and premiums. In court, the analyst with the best empirical evidence to support his or her position usually wins, so the analyst should be thoroughly familiar with the data on discounts for lack of marketability.

The next most frequent discount issue is minority interest, commonly referred to as lack of control. The courts also have recognized at least half a dozen other categories of discounts. This is one of the most important chapters in the *Business Valuation Body of Knowledge*.

MULTIPLE CHOICE QUESTIONS

1. The guideline public company method produces what type of value?

   a. Synergistic

   b. Control

   c. Marketable minority

   d. Nonmarketable minority

2. From 1998 through 2001, what percentage of takeovers of public companies occurred at a price below the immediately previous public market trading price?

   a. Over 15%

   b. 10–15%

   c. 5–10%

   d. Less than 5%

3. All of the following have been demonstrated to be factors influencing the magnitude of the discount for lack of marketability EXCEPT:

   a. Dividends or withdrawals

   b. The perceived liquidity event (e.g., buyout or public offering)

   c. The absolute size of the block

   d. The size of the block relative to the total stock outstanding

4. Which of the following sometimes is used to help quantify a discount for minority interest?

   a. SEC Institutional Investor Study

   b. Columbia Financial Advisors Study

   c. *Mergerstat/Shannon Pratt's Control Premium Study*™

   d. Standard Research Consultants Study

5. Which of the following is a correct statement about discounts for trapped-in capital gains taxes on appreciated assets?

   a. Since the *Davis* case in 1998, the U.S. Tax Court sometimes has recognized a discount for trapped-in capital gains and in some cases has not; the same is true for family law courts.

   b. Since the *Davis* case in 1998, the U.S. Tax Court has consistently recognized a discount for trapped-in capital gains taxes, and most family law courts have done the same.

   c. Since the *Davis* case in 1998, the U.S. Tax Court has consistently recognized a discount for trapped-in capital gains, but most family law courts have held that trapped-in capital gains are recognizable only if a sale is imminent.

   d. Neither the U.S. Tax Court nor family law courts recognize discounts for trapped-in capital gains taxes on the basis that such taxes are speculative.

6. Which is the most comprehensive restricted stock study in terms of amount of information disclosed for each transaction?

   a. SEC Institutional Investor Study

   b. *The FMV Restricted Stock Study*™

   c. Silber Study

   d. Management Planning Study

7. Which pre-IPO discount for lack of marketability studies had the most (over 2,000) transactions as of mid-2002?

   a. John Emory (formerly Baird & Co.) Studies

   b. Willamette Management Associates Studies

   c. *Valuation Advisors' Lack of Marketability Discount Study*™

   d. None of the above

8. What is the number of the Revenue Ruling that recognizes restricted stock studies as evidence of lack of marketability?

   a. 68-609

   b. 77-287

   c. 83-120

   d. 93-12

TRUE OR FALSE QUESTIONS

9. When valuing very small minority interests, and large amounts of both voting and nonvoting stock are outstanding, there may be little or no appreciable difference between voting and nonvoting stock values.   True   False

10. The U.S. Tax Court sometimes allows a discount for the loss of a key person in estate tax cases.   True   False

11. Since 1986 all new employee stock ownership plans (ESOPs) have been required to have "put" rights for withdrawing stockholders, which can reduce or even eliminate the discount for lack of marketability.   True   False

12. Minority stockholders are eligible to register a company's stock for a public offering.   True   False

FILL-IN-THE-BLANK QUESTIONS

13. A discount to reflect a group of dissimilar operations or assets that may not be as attractive to investors as single operations or a group of similar operations is referred to as a _____ discount.

14. A discount to reflect the fact that the number of shares of stock is so large that the market may take a long time to absorb it without depressing the price is called:

_____ .

EXERCISE

15. If a stock is valued at $12 per share on a control basis and a 20% lack of control discount and a 40% lack of marketability discount are applied, what is the minority nonmarketable value per share?

Chapter 17

Reconciliation and Value Conclusion

Once valuation methods have been performed and indications of value reached, it is time to decide on the final value conclusion. Sometimes one method will dominate and thus be accorded 100% of the weight. At other times some weight will be accorded to each of two or more indications of value from different methods. This is when analytical judgment comes into play. No hard-and-fast empirical tests exist, but there are some general guidelines.

MULTIPLE CHOICE QUESTIONS

1. In reconciling various indications of value for a holding company, which of the following probably should be accorded the *least* weight?

   a. Adjusted net asset value (asset approach)

   b. Price/book value (market approach)

   c. Price/adjusted book value (market approach)

   d. Price/earnings (market approach)

2. For which of the following broad industry groups are asset values usually accorded the most weight?

   a. Distribution companies

   b. Service companies

   c. Professional practices

   d. Manufacturing companies

TRUE OR FALSE QUESTIONS

3. IRS Revenue Rulings have the force of law.   True   False

4. The "Delaware Block Method" uses mathematical weightings of various factors and is still acceptable provided the analyst demonstrates that all relevant factors have been considered and reflected if appropriate.   True   False

5. Within the market approach, the most weight generally should be accorded to value multiples with the highest coefficients of variation.   True   False

PART IV
Analysis
of the Company

Chapter 18

Financial Statement Analysis

There are two aspects to financial statement analysis: adjusting the statements and analyzing them for trends and ratios. These adjusted statements then are used in all approaches to valuation. The trend and ratio analysis is used as a basis for projections and discount rates in the income approach and for developing applicable multiples in the market approach.

MULTIPLE CHOICE QUESTIONS

1. Normalizing adjustments:
   I.   Present data using generally accepted accounting principles (GAAP)
   II. Present data using industry accounting standards
   III. Bring assets and/or liabilities to their respective fair market values
   IV. Eliminate nonrecurring items
   V.   Provide a foundation for developing future expectations about the subject company

   a. I, II, III

   b. I, II, IV, V

   c. II, III, V

   d. II, III, IV, V

   e. I, II, III, IV, V

2. Which of the following are activity ratios?
   I.   Fixed assets to equity
   II. Inventory turnover
   III. Times interest earned
   IV. Sales to total assets
   V.   Sales to networking capital

   a. I, III, IV

   b. II, III, IV

   c. I, IV, V

   d. II, IV, V

   e. III, IV, V

3. Which of the following are leverage ratios?

   I.   Equity to total assets
   II.   Long-term debt to total capital
   III. Total liabilities to total assets
   IV.   Sales to fixed assets
   V.   Times interest earned

       a. I, II, III

       b. II, III, V

       c. II, III, IV

       d. I, III, V

       e. I, III, IV

4. Which of the following are liquidity ratios?

   I.   Debt to tangible equity
   II.   Current ratio
   III. Times interest earned
   IV.   Coverage of fixed charges
   V.   Equity to total capital

       a. I, II, IV

       b. I, III, V

       c. I, II, III

       d. II, III, IV

       e. III, IV, V

5. The coefficient of variation is calculated as:

   a. Median/standard deviation

   b. Mean/standard deviation

   c. Standard deviation/median

   d. Standard deviation/mean

   e. Standard deviation/mode

6. Examples of control adjustments are:

   I.   Litigation cost, payments, or recoveries

   II. Discontinued operations

   III. Elimination of operational inefficiencies and excess costs

   IV. Changes in transactions involving company insiders

     a. I, IV

     b. III, IV

     c. II, III

     d. II, III, IV

TRUE OR FALSE QUESTIONS

7. An activity ratio relates an income statement variable to a balance sheet variable.   True   False

8. The general purpose of a balance sheet leverage ratio is to aid in quantifiable assessment of the long-term solvency of the business and its ability to deal with financial problems and opportunities as they arise.   True   False

EXERCISES

Use the following information to answer questions 9 through 13.

Optimum Devices
Consolidated Balance Sheet as of September 30, 2002

Assets
   Current Assets

Cash	$ 59,847
Short-term Investments	$ 251,764
Accounts Receivable	$ 3,196,831
Inventory	$ 4,129,524
Total Current Assets	$ 7,637,966
Long-term Assets	
Property and Equipment	$ 3,689,345
Investment in Affiliate	$ 335,585
Goodwill: Net	$ 48,863
Total Long-term Assets	$ 4,073,793
Total Assets	$11,711,759

Liabilities and Stockholder's Equity
    Current Liabilities

Accounts Payable	$ 1,916,441
Short-term Borrowings	$ 1,830,000
Current Portion of Long-term Debt	$ 304,786
Total Current Liabilities	$ 4,051,227
Long-term Liabilities	
Long-term Debt	$ 1,341,012
Total Long-term Liabilities	$ 1,341,012
Stockholder's Equity	
Paid-in Capital	$ 2,938,818
Retained Earnings	$ 3,380,702
Total Stockholder's Equity	$ 6,319,520
Total Liabilities and Stockholder's Equity	$11,711,759

Optimum Devices
Consolidated Statements of Income for the Year Ended September 30, 2002

Sales: Net	$13,243,801
Cost of Goods Sold	$ 7,946,744
Gross Profit	$ 5,297,057
Selling, General, and Administrative Expenses	$ 3,669,671
Operating Income	$ 1,627,386
Interest Expense	$ 261,212
Earnings Before Taxes	$ 1,366,174
Taxes	$ 323,293
Net Income	$ 1,042,881

Notes:
SG&A includes $258,562 depreciation and amortization.
Financial statements are adapted from Taylor Devices, Incorporated's 8/28/2001 10-K filing.

9. What is the inventory turnover?

10. What is the return on investment?

11. What is the current ratio?

12. What is the quick ratio?

13. What is the times interest earned?

Chapter 19

Using Economic and Industry Data

No company operates in a vacuum. Different companies are impacted by different macro-economic and microeconomic forces. The analyst needs to determine which economic forces impact the subject company and where to find information on the history and outlook for those forces.

Similarly, industry forces impact companies, and the analyst needs to identify those industry forces and where to get information on the history and outlook for those forces.

Comparing the company with its peers in the industry should reveal relative strengths and weaknesses, which should help in assessing risk and growth potential, thus providing a basis for selecting discount and capitalization rates and market multiples.

Finally, industry data may provide a source for reasonable compensation, probably the most frequent income statement adjustment.

MULTIPLE CHOICE QUESTIONS

1. Which of the following general industry composite data sources is compiled from bank loan department documents?

   a. Risk Management Association's (formerly Robert Morris Associates) *Annual Statement Studies*

   b. Financial Research Associates' *Financial Studies of the Small Business*

   c. *Financial Ratio Analyst*

   d. *Almanac of Business and Industrial Financial Ratios*

2. All of the following sources are based on tax return data EXCEPT:

   a. *Corporation Source Book*

   b. *IRS Corporate Ratios*

   c. *Survey of Current Business*

   d. *Almanac of Business and Industrial Financial Ratios*

3. Industry composite information falls largely into which three of the following categories:

   I.   On-site management interviews

   II. General industry sources

   III. Compilations from tax returns

   IV. Trade association or trade magazine compilations

   V.   University research centers

       a. I, II, III

       b. II, III, IV

       c. II, III, V

       d. II, IV, V

4. Primary sources of regional economic data include all of the following EXCEPT:

   a. Bank economic departments

   b. Chambers of commerce

   c. *Federal Reserve Bulletin*

   d. Public utilities

5. Sources of national economic data include all of the following EXCEPT:

   a. *Survey of Buying Power*

   b. *Federal Reserve Bulletin*

   c. *Economic Report of the President*

   d. *Statistical Abstract of the United States*

6. All of the following are national sources that provide data by region EXCEPT:

   a. *Survey of Buying Power*

   b. *The Complete Economic and Demographic Data Source*

   c. *Metro Insights*

   d. *Survey of Current Business*

TRUE OR FALSE QUESTIONS

7. The most frequent income statement adjustment found in valuations
   on a controlling interest basis is for nonoperating income.   True   False

8. *Financial Statements of the Small Business* contains information on
   companies with less than $1 million in sales or assets and is compiled
   from tax returns.   True   False

9. In addition to publications providing compensation data, proxy
   statements of public guideline companies are good sources of
   compensation data.   True   False

Chapter 20

Site Visits and Interviews

Visiting a company site or sites and interviewing its management can be one of the most interesting and pleasurable steps in the valuation. In most cases, the site visits and management interviews will reveal aspects of the company that the analyst had not even thought about. A better understanding of the company can impact the value conclusion and also give the analyst confidence in the final conclusion.

MULTIPLE CHOICE QUESTION

1. The general objectives of site visits and management interviews are to:

   I.   Gain an understanding of the company and its operations
   II. Explain the fee structure for your valuation assignment
   III. Identify the company's strengths and weaknesses
   IV. Understand where the company fits in the industry

   a. I, II, IV

   b. I, III, IV

   c. II, III, IV

   d. I, II, III, IV

TRUE OR FALSE QUESTIONS

2. During the site visit and management interview, the analyst needs to understand what additional investment will be required to support the projected operations so he or she can value the returns on future investments.   True   False

3. It is best to perform the preliminary financial statement analysis during the on-site interview so any questions can be answered then.   True   False

4. Subsequent events that affect value between the effective date and the date the report is issued normally would not be considered, but the analyst may wish to consult the client's attorney regarding possible exceptions to the general rule.   True   False

FILL-IN-THE-BLANK QUESTIONS

5. List four items an analyst might choose to investigate during a site visit, specifically regarding the physical operation:

   _____

   _____

   _____

   _____

6. List five areas of inquiry to be investigated during a site visit and interview.

   _____

   _____

   _____

   _____

   _____

PART V
Supporting Data

Chapter 21

Sources of Supporting Data

Every valuation engagement and report can be broken down into specific steps, such as describing the economic outlook, estimating the cost of capital, forecasting sales, and so on. In each of these steps, the appraiser has to use various types of data to reach and support the opinion of value. At the same time, a business cannot be valued in isolation of its competition or the general business environment. When valuing a business, the appraiser must look further than the subject company's financial statements and consider external factors that affect the way the company will perform and thus its value.

MULTIPLE CHOICE QUESTIONS

1. All of the following are sources of cost of capital data EXCEPT:

   a. Ibbotson Associates' *Cost of Capital Yearbook*

   b. *Stocks, Bonds, Bills, and Inflation® Yearbook*

   c. Ibbotson Associates' Cost of Capital Center Web site

   d. COMPUSTAT

2. Ibbotson Associates is known mainly as a source for:

   a. Earnings forecasts and related data

   b. Guideline public company data

   c. Cost of capital data

   d. Guideline merger and acquisition data

3. *Mergerstat/Shannon Pratt's Control Premium Study*™ is a source for:

   I.   Cost of capital data

   II. Arbitrage pricing theory data

   III. Guideline merger and acquisition data

   IV. Minority discount and control premium data

     a. III

     b. I, III

     c. II, III

     d. III, IV

4. Moody's is known primarily as a source for:

     a. Cost of capital data

     b. Guideline public company data

     c. Earnings forecasts and related data

     d. Merged or acquired public company data

5. The most comprehensive source of free public company data is:

     a. EDGAR

     b. Peerscape

     c. Compact DISEC

     d. COMPUSTAT

6. All of the following are sources of earnings forecasts and related data EXCEPT:

   I.   Ibbotson Associates

   II. *Value Line Investment Survey*

   III. *BIRR Risks and Returns Analyzer*®

   IV. I/B/E/S United States Database

     a. I

     b. II, IV

     c. III

     d. I, III

7. The main sources of data for merged or acquired private companies are:

    a. BIZCOMPS®, *Pratt's Stats*™, *IBA Market Database*, and *Mergerstat/Shannon Pratt's Control Premium Study*™

    b. *Done Deals*®, *IBA Market Database*, *Pratt's Stats*™, and *Mergerstat/Shannon Pratt's Control Premium Study*™

    c. *Mergerstat/Shannon Pratt's Control Premium Study*™, *Pratt's Stats*™, and *Done Deals*®

    d. BIZCOMPS®, *Done Deals*®, *IBA Market Database*, and *Pratt's Stats*™

8. All of the following are sources of performance data EXCEPT:

    a. *Industry Norms and Key Business Ratios*

    b. *Economic Report of the President*

    c. *Standard & Poor's Industry Reports*

    d. *Almanac of Business and Industrial Financial Ratios*

TRUE OR FALSE QUESTIONS

9. *Pratt's Stats*™ is a source of public company data.   True   False

10. *Mergerstat/Shannon Pratt's Control Premium Study*™ and *Mergerstat*® *Review* offer the same type of data.   True   False

11. Generally, the same source of data will offer data on both public and private companies.   True   False

12. Sources of compensation data have limited application in appraisal reports.   True   False

13. Federal Reserve Banks are generally all excellent resources of national economic data.   True   False

14. *Census of Manufacturers*, *Census of Wholesale Trade*, and *Census of Service Industries* are sources of regional and local economic data.   True   False

FILL-IN-THE-BLANK QUESTIONS

15. The SEC Institutional Investor Study is a source of data for

_____ .

16. The Emory Studies (previously Baird & Co. Studies) are compilations of
_____ transaction data
and are used to quantify _____ .

17. The *U.S. Industry and Trade Outlook* is a widely used source for
_____ data.

PART VI
Valuations for Specific Purposes

Chapter 22

Tax-Related Valuations

Many appraisals are done for tax-related purposes, and Revenue Ruling (RR) 59-60, which applies to the valuation of common stock, is probably the most widely quoted piece of literature in the business valuation field. Many appraisers reread RR 59-60 every six months or so to be sure they are aware of all of its nuances. RR 68-609 notes that RR 59-60 is also applicable to partnerships and sole proprietorship interests.

MULTIPLE CHOICE QUESTIONS

1. What is the standard of value for most tax-related valuations?

    a. Fair market value

    b. Fair value

    c. Intrinsic value

    d. Investment value

2. All of the following are listed in Revenue Ruling 59-60 among the eight basic factors to consider EXCEPT:

    a. The dividend-paying capacity of the company

    b. Whether the company is dependent on a key person

    c. Whether the enterprise has goodwill or other intangible value

    d. The market prices of stock of corporations engaged in the same or similar line of business having their stocks actively traded in a free and open market

3. Even if section 2701 of Internal Revenue Code chapter 14 applies to a transfer of an interest in a family-controlled company, all of the following features will provide a basis for attributing value to the retained senior securities EXCEPT:

    a. Cumulative dividend or distribution right

    b. Mandatory redemption rights that require the retained senior security interests to receive a certain amount on a specific date

    c. An option to acquire equity interests

    d. Nonlapsing conversion rights that give the senior securities the right to be converted into a stated number of shares or percentage of the same class as the transferred interest

4. According to Revenue Ruling 66-49, which applies to appraisals of charitable contributions of noncash property for federal income tax purposes, the stated requirements for being qualified as an appraiser include all of the following EXCEPT:

   a. Being certified by one or more recognized professional appraisal organizations as being qualified to appraise the subject category of property

   b. Holding oneself out to the public as an appraiser who regularly performs appraisals

   c. Being qualified to appraise property because of one's qualifications

   d. Being aware of the appraiser penalties associated with the overvaluation of charitable contributions

TRUE OR FALSE QUESTIONS

5. Revenue Ruling 59-60 states that "valuation of securities is, in essence, a prophesy as to the future, and must be based on the facts available at the required date of appraisal."   True   False

6. Section 2703 of Internal Revenue Code chapter 14 effectively prevents a fixed price in a buy-sell agreement entered into after 1990 from determining value for estate tax purposes.   True   False

7. Under section 2704 of Internal Revenue Code chapter 14, the analyst is required to ignore restrictions that are more restrictive than those found under the applicable state law.   True   False

8. The appraisal summary, made on Form 8283 (noncash charitable contributions), requires *all* of the following: True   False

   a. Signed and dated by donee
   b. Signed and dated by qualified appraiser
   c. Must be attached to the donor's return on which a deduction for the appraised property is first claimed or reported

Chapter 23

Employee Stock Ownership Plans

There are over 12,000 employee stock ownership plans (ESOPs) in the United States, and they provide a substantial amount of work for business appraisers. Increasingly, professional business appraisal organizations tend to include ESOP appraisal in their curricula and to test for knowledge of them in their certifying exams.

MULTIPLE CHOICE QUESTIONS

1. All of the following are correct characterizations of ESOP stock EXCEPT:

   a. The employees must have the option to sell (put) their stock to the ESOP following retirement, disability, or termination, at the ESOP stock's appraised value.

   b. Qualifying contributions are tax-deductible to the corporation, whether made in cash or stock.

   c. ESOPs can own any amount of the company's stock—from a tiny percentage up to 100%.

   d. Both S and C corporations can have ESOPs.

2. Which of the following is a correct statement about tax deductibility to the corporation of dividends paid on ESOP stock?

   a. The dividends are tax-deductible if used to pay ESOP debt, but not if passed through to participants.

   b. The dividends are tax-deductible to the corporation if passed through to participants, but not if used to pay ESOP debt.

   c. Dividends are tax-deductible if they are *either* used to pay ESOP debt or passed through to participants.

   d. Dividends are not tax-deductible to the corporation regardless of the purpose for which they are used.

3. How much stock must the ESOP own after the transaction for the seller to get a tax-free rollover under Internal Revenue Code section 1042?

   a. There is no minimum requirement.

   b. 20%

   c. 30%

   d. 50%

TRUE OR FALSE QUESTIONS

4. If the ESOP owns 100% of the company's stock, the valuation must be done on a control basis.   True   False

5. The Department of Labor (DOL) proposed regulations (which were never finalized but nevertheless are used as guidance for ESOP valuations) define *fair market value* slightly differently from the Treasury regulations.   True   False

6. The proposed DOL regulation requires that marketability, or lack thereof, be addressed as a relevant factor.   True   False

7. The appraiser is a fiduciary to the ESOP.   True   False

8. In leveraged ESOPs, amounts paid to principal as well as interest are tax-deductible to the corporation.   True   False

9. Dividends received on ESOP stock are tax-free to participants. True   False

FILL-IN-THE-BLANK QUESTIONS

10. ESOPs are subject to ERISA. What do the initials ERISA stand for?

    _____

11. List four of the parties or agencies that pose potential challenges to an ESOP stock valuation:

    _____

    _____

    _____

    _____

12. The put option creates what for the company, which must be addressed by the appraiser as a risk factor.

_____

Chapter 24

Shareholder Buyouts and Disputes

Shareholder buyouts are a growing reason for professional business valuations. These buyouts arise largely in two distinct (but related) categories: dissenting stockholder suits (where minority stockholders dissent to a merger or other corporate action giving rise to dissenting stockholder appraisal rights) and minority oppression suits.

MULTIPLE CHOICE QUESTIONS

1. Which is a correct statement about the states' precedential case law regarding minority and marketability discounts in dissenting stockholder cases?

   a. Most states have case law disallowing either minority or marketability discounts.

   b. Most states have case law disallowing minority discounts but allowing marketability discounts.

   c. Most states have case law disallowing marketability discounts but allowing minority discounts.

   d. There is no consensus for "most states"; those that have case law on these issues are mixed and some have no case law on these issues.

2. Which of the following is typical of the Delaware courts regarding minority and marketability discounts in dissenting stockholder cases?

   a. They typically allow both.

   b. They typically allow minority discounts but not marketability discounts.

   c. They typically allow marketability discounts but not minority discounts.

   d. They typically do not allow either minority or marketability discounts.

3. What is the current posture of Delaware courts regarding the preferred method of valuation for dissenting stockholder actions?

   a. They have expressed a preference for the discounted cash flow method.

   b. They have expressed a preference for the capitalized cash flow method.

   c. They have expressed a preference for the guideline public company method.

   d. They have expressed a preference for the guideline merged and acquired company method.

4. What is the typical standard of value for most minority oppression dissolution actions?

   a. Fair market value

   b. Fair value

   c. Investment value

   d. Intrinsic value

5. What is the standard of value in *most* bankruptcy reorganizations?

   a. Fair market value

   b. Fair value

   c. Investment value

   d. Intrinsic value

6. What is the standard of value for buy-sell agreements?

   a. Fair market value

   b. Fair value

   c. Investment value

   d. Anything to which the parties willingly commit

TRUE OR FALSE QUESTIONS

7. All states allow controlling stockholders to take actions such as mergers or reverse stock splits that cause minority stockholders to be bought out, either in cash or in stock of another company.   True   False

8. Under the minority oppression statutes in most states that have such statutes, the control stockholders may choose to buy out the minority stockholders at appraised value under the statute.   True   False

9. Bankruptcy courts recognize all three of the traditional appraisal approaches (income, market, and asset-based).   True   False

FILL-IN-THE-BLANK QUESTIONS

10. A procedure that assigns percentage weights to the results of each of several approaches to value in dissenting stockholder suits is known as:

    _____ .

11. In a bankruptcy reorganization, the premise of value is often a major issue that can greatly affect a trustee's or court's acceptance or rejection of a proposed plan of reorganization. What are the two major premises of value?

    _____

    _____

Chapter 25

Marital Dissolutions

Probably the largest single category of professional business valuations, at least in terms of number of assignments, is marital dissolutions. Sadly, it is probably the category characterized by some of the worst business valuation practices.

More cases are remanded to the trial court from the appellate level for insufficient valuation evidence in marital dissolution cases than in all other categories of cases combined. Moreover, most family law judges are less familiar with business valuation than judges typically hearing any other major category of cases (e.g., tax, dissenting stockholder, bankruptcy reorganization, etc.), so case decisions often do not provide good guidance to the appraiser on valuation issues.

MULTIPLE CHOICE QUESTIONS

1. Which of the following, if any, is the typical statutory standard of value in most states for marital dissolution?

   a. Fair market value

   b. Fair value

   c. Intrinsic value

   d. None

2. What are the states' postures toward goodwill as marital property?

   a. Its value is seldom distributed as a marital asset.

   b. The value of entity or practice goodwill *only* is a distributable marital asset.

   c. All intangible value in the nature of goodwill (both personal and entity goodwill) is distributable.

   d. Each of the above typifies the postures of some states.

3. What are typical postures of family law courts' on discounts for trapped-in capital gains taxes on appreciated property?

   a. They typically have allowed such discounts.

   b. They never have allowed such discounts.

   c. Before 1998 they usually did not allow such discounts, but in light of the *Davis* case in the U.S. Tax Court, in recent years they usually have allowed such discounts.

   d. They have been reluctant to allow such discounts unless a sale of the property is imminent or the tax will be triggered as a result of the court's decision.

TRUE OR FALSE QUESTIONS

4. Marital dissolutions are one of the leading reasons for valuing
   businesses and professional practices.   True   False

5. Most states' case law for marital dissolutions follows the standard of
   fair market value relatively closely.   True   False

6. For marital dissolution purposes, the valuation date is the date of trial.   True   False

7. Family law courts fairly consistently apply discounts for minority
   interest and lack of marketability when applicable.   True   False

8. The analyst having difficulty obtaining cooperation during discovery
   in a marital dissolution case can advise the attorney that case law
   broadly supports the proposition that the nonoperating spouse has a
   financial interest in the property and is entitled to all of the
   information available to the operating spouse.   True   False

SECTION TWO
Answers

PART I
Business Valuation
Engagement Environment

Business Valuation Legal and Regulatory Environment

ANSWERS

Multiple Choice Questions

1. d. ESOPs are governed by the Employee Retirement Income Security Act (ERISA).
2. b. 68-609 (also called the "formula method").
3. d. Reverses RR 81-283. Minority stockholder of a family-controlled company is *not* subject to family attribution.
4. c

True or False Questions

5. True.
6. True.
7. True, but it may be cited in support of a position.
8. True.
9. False. Revenue Rulings express the positions of the IRS, but courts are not bound by them.
10. False. There can be different values for the same share of stock in different legal contexts. For example, when valuing a minority interest in closely held stock for gift or estate tax purposes, both minority and marketability discounts usually are applicable; but when valuing an interest for dissenting stockholder actions, whether the same discounts are applicable depends on precedential case law in the jurisdiction.
11. True. The revised guidelines were published in the fall of 2001, and they are available for free downloading at *BVLibrary.com^{sm}*, including a report checklist.

Fill-in-the-Blank Question

12. Field Service Advice Memorandums (FSAs)

Chapter 2

Business Valuation Professional Environment

ANSWERS

Multiple Choice Questions

1. c. Its membership is comprised solely of professional appraisal organizations, not individuals, and it is funded by member organizations, Congress, and donations.

2. a

3. a

4. b

5. d

6. a

True or False Questions

7. True

8. True

Fill-in-the-Blank Questions

9. *Uniform Standards of Professional Appraisal Practice (USPAP)*

10. a. Center for Advanced Valuation Studies

    b. American Society of Appraisers

Chapter 3

Business Valuation Engagement

ANSWERS

Multiple Choice Questions

1. b. No or almost no states address the issue of minority or marketability discounts in their statutes. States' positions on this issue must be gleaned from case law, if any.

2. d. Analysts have only case law for guidance in marital dissolution.

3. b. But state case law does not necessarily define fair value the same way for dissenting shareholder actions and minority oppression actions.

4. b. Transaction value is the face value at which an actual transaction occurred. It usually *does* impound motivations or circumstances of the specific buyer and/or seller, such as synergies or compulsion.

5. d

6. c. The dollar amount of the fee or fee arrangements usually are not spelled out, but the certification usually contains language indicating that the fee was not contingent on any conclusion or outcome.

True or False Questions

7. False. Fair value is defined in SFAS 142 as "the amount at which an asset (or liability) could be bought (or incurred) or sold (or settled) in a current transaction between willing parties, that is, other than in a forced or liquidation sale."

8. True. This is a good opportunity for appraisers to identify intangible elements of value so that the client can save taxes by subtracting intangible elements of value from the total value.

9. True. If your standard engagement letter does not have an indemnification clause, you should include one immediately. Lawsuits naming appraisers as defendants are on the rise.

10. True. Clients do not like surprises.

11. False. In fact, the appraiser may request a representation letter from the client, the company, or an attorney verifying the accuracy of some or all of the factual material and/or assumptions on which the appraiser relied.

12. True. Lack of timely receipt of information is the single worst problem in appraisers meeting their schedules. If information is not forthcoming on a timely basis, the appraiser should notify the client, preferably in writing, that lack of information jeopardizes timely completion of the engagement.

13. True. If your standard engagement letter does not have such a statement, include one immediately. Many appraisers have been sued by clients using the valuation for an unintended purpose or for a different valuation date.

Fill-in-the-Blank Questions

14. Investment value

15. Intrinsic value

Chapter 4

Litigation Service Engagements

ANSWERS

Multiple Choice Questions

1. b
2. c
3. a

True or False Questions

4. False. A *bench trial* is a trial without a jury, and the judge has the final authority including issuing the findings of fact.

5. True. Some judges construe the type of evidence that experts normally rely on more broadly or narrowly than others.

6. True.

7. True, but there are some exceptions. For example, New York, which is one of the most confusing, has three levels, but some of its trial courts are called supreme courts, and its highest court is called the court of appeals.

8. True.

Fill-in-the-Blank Questions

9. Federal Rules of Evidence
10. Voir dire

PART II
Terminology and Notation

International Glossary of Business Valuation Terms

ANSWERS

Multiple Choice Questions

1. d. The arbitrage pricing model is a multiple regression model that incorporates several economic variables, one of which may or may not be beta (usually macroeconomic variables and not beta).

2. d. In the hierarchy of valuation terminology, the broadest term is approach (income, market, asset); the next level is method (e.g., the discounting method and the capitalization method are under the income approach); and the third level is procedure (e.g., the build-up model for estimating an equity discount rate within the discounting method).

3. a. Beta

4. c. Investment value

True or False Questions

5. False. The current cost of an identical new property is called *reproduction cost. Replacement cost* is the current cost of a property having the nearest equivalent utility to the property being valued.

6. True.

7. True.

8. True.

Fill-in-the-Blank Questions

9. Common size statements

10. Internal rate of return

Chapter 6

Notation System Used in This Book

ANSWERS

Multiple Choice Questions

1. a

2. a. The Standard & Poor's 500 Index (S&P 500) is the most widely used benchmark for the "market," so the risk premium for the market is usually measured as the difference in returns between the risk-free rate and the S&P 500.

3. b

4. c. Tax rate (usually expressed as a percentage of pretax income)

True or False Questions

5. False. When computing a WACC, it is assumed that the relative weights of the components are at *market* value, not book value.

6. False. The letter k stands for discount rate, or the total cost of capital for a given class. The symbol for capitalization rate is c, which means direct capitalization (dividing one number by the denominator c).

Fill-in-the-Blank Questions

7. Earnings Before Interest, Taxes, Depreciation, and Amortization

8. Market Value of Invested Capital

PART III
Valuation Approaches and Methods

Chapter 7

Overview of Valuation Approaches and Methods

ANSWERS

Multiple Choice Questions

1. a

2. d

3. c. There are no statutory standards of value for marital dissolutions in most states. To learn the accepted standard of value in a given jurisdiction, the analyst must study the case law in that jurisdiction.

True or False Questions

4. True.

5. True.

6. False. Often the term *fair market value* is used in opinions in marital dissolution cases when procedures used are not consistent with the standard of fair market value as defined in this book and as interpreted by the U.S. Tax Court. For example, family law courts often include elements of *investment value* (value to a specific person) and then label the result fair market value.

7. True.

Fill-in-the-Blank Questions

8. a. Income
   b. Market
   c. Asset

9. a. Methods
   b. Procedures

10. Invested capital

Chapter 8

Income Approach: Cost of Capital

ANSWERS

Multiple Choice Questions

1. a. It is not what the company *can* pay; it is what the market *requires*.

2. d

3. c. The nominal rate of return in b. and the risk-free rate in d. already incorporate inflation expectations.

4. d

5. b

6. b

7. b. The cost of capital is a function of the investment, is based on market prices, and is based on investors' expectations.

8. d

9. b

10. b

11. c

12. d

13. c. Dividends to preferred or common equity investors are not tax-deductible, so the costs of common and preferred equity are not computed on a pretax or after-tax basis.

14. b

15. b

16. a

17. c

18. d

19. c

20. d

True or False Questions

21. True.

22. True.

23. False. The minority stockholder has no power to change the capital structure; therefore, when valuing a minority interest, the actual capital structure usually is used.

24. False. The risk-free rate and the equity risk premium are two distinct components of the cost of equity capital.

25. False. It is the general risk premium that is multiplied by beta in CAPM. The result is the specific equity risk premium for the subject company.

26. False. Betas are estimated from historical market returns. Since private companies do not have historical stock prices, betas cannot be computed directly.

27. False.

Fill-in-the-Blank Questions

28. Substitution

29. Risk

30. Weighted average cost of capital (WACC)

31. Risks

32. Beta

33. After; before

Exercises

34. The 6% after-tax cost of debt is computed as $K_d = K_{d(pt)}(1 - t) = 0.10 \times (1 - .40) = 0.06$ or 6%.

35. To compute WACC, we use the following formula, using market values for weights:

$$WACC = (K_e \times W_e) + (K_p \times W_p) + (K_{d(pt)}[(1 - t) \times W_d]$$

Or we can present the formula in a tabular form:

Capital Component	Amount of Capital Component	% of Capital Component in Capital Structure	Cost of Capital Component	Weighted Cost of Capital Component
Debt	$ 500,000	14%	6%	0.84%
Preferred Equity	$1,000,000	29%	15%	4.35%
Common Equity	$2,000,000	57%	20%	11.40%
	$3,500,000	100%		
	Weighted Average Cost of Capital			16.59%

36. To solve this we apply the Capital Asset Pricing Model:

$$E(R_i) = R_f + B(RP_m)$$

In our case:

$$E(R_i) = 6.25\% + 0.75(5.5\%)$$
$$= 10.38\%$$

37. The formula for relevering beta is:

$$B_L = B_U[1 + (1 - t)(W_d / W_e)]$$

In our case:

$$B_L = 0.80[1 + (1 - 0.4)(0.40 / 0.60)]$$
$$= 1.12$$

38. The formula for the unlevered beta is:

$$B_U = \frac{B_L}{1 + (1 - t)(W_d / W_e)}$$

$$= \frac{1.25}{1 + (1 - 0.4)(0.4 / 0.6)}$$

$$= 0.89$$

39. The formula for the single-stage DCF model is:

$$PV = \frac{NCF_0(1 + g)}{k - g}$$

In our case:

$$PV = \frac{\$1,000,000(1 + 0.10)}{0.20 - 0.10}$$

$$= \$11,000,000$$

Income Approach: Discounting Method

ANSWERS

Multiple Choice Questions

1. a
2. d
3. b
4. c

True or False Questions

5. False.
6. True.
7. False.
8. False. This is a common error. The terminal value is the value at the *beginning* of the year following the discrete projection period and, therefore, should be discounted for *n* years—the same as the last year in the discrete projection period.
9. False. It depends primarily on the numerator (the projected cash flows) rather than on the denominator (the discount rate).
10. True.

Fill-in-the-Blank Questions

11. Common equity; invested capital
12. Cost of equity capital; weighted average cost of capital (WACC)

Exercises

13. The net cash flow to equity is defined and computed as:

Net income	$1,000,000
+ Noncash charges	$ 200,000
− Capital expenditures	$ 300,000
− Additions to working capital	$ 100,000
+ New debt incurred	$ 200,000
− Debt repayments	$ 100,000
= Net cash flow to equity	$ 900,000

14. The net cash flow to invested capital is defined and computed as:

Net income	$1,000,000
+ Noncash charges	$ 200,000
− Capital expenditures	$ 300,000
− Additions to working capital	$ 100,000
+ Interest expense	$ 50,000
= Net cash flow to invested capital	$ 850,000

15.
$$PV = \frac{NCF_1}{(1+k)} + \frac{NCF_2}{(1+k)^2} + \ldots + \frac{NCF_n}{(1+k)^n}$$

$$= \frac{\$100}{(1+0.10)} + \frac{\$100}{(1+0.10)^2} + \frac{\$1,100}{(1+0.10)^3}$$

$$= \$90.91 + \$82.64 + \$827.07 = \$1,000.62$$

Because the fair market value of this investment, $1,000.62, is higher than its cost today, $950, this would be a good investment opportunity.

16. We present the answer to this in tabular format:

Amount	Probability of Occurrence	Weighted Value
$1,000	10%	$ 100
$1,100	15%	$ 165
$1,200	45%	$ 540
$1,300	15%	$ 195
$1,400	15%	$ 210
	100%	**$1,210**

Because the expected value of the probability-weighted distribution is different from the most likely cash flow, this is a skewed distribution.

17.
$$PV = \frac{NCF_1}{(1+k)^{0.5}} + \frac{NCF_2}{(1+k)^{1.5}} + \ldots + \frac{NCF_n}{(1+k)^{n-0.5}}$$

$$PV = \frac{\$100}{(1+0.10)^{0.5}} + \frac{\$100}{(1+0.10)^{1.5}} + \frac{\$1,100}{(1+0.10)^{2.5}}$$

In our case:

This value is higher than the resulting value if the year-end discounting convention were used.

$$= \frac{\$100}{1.05} + \frac{\$100}{1.15} + \frac{\$1,100}{1.27}$$

$$= \$95.24 + \$86.96 + \$866.14$$

$$= \$1,048.34$$

Given that the fair market value of the cash flow series is higher than its cost today, this would be a profitable investment opportunity.

Chapter 10

Income Approach: Capitalization Method

ANSWERS

Multiple Choice Questions

1. b
2. b
3. c
4. d
5. b

True or False Questions

6. True.
7. False.
8. False.
9. True.

Fill-in-the-Blank Questions

10. Capitalization
11. Net cash flow
12. Terminal value or residual value

Exercises

13. $PV = \dfrac{NCF_1}{c}$

    In our case:

    $PV = \dfrac{\$4}{0.08}$

    $= \$50.00$

    The fair market value of the underlying investment is $50. This is the amount a willing buyer would expect to pay and a willing seller would expect to receive.

14. $PV = \dfrac{NCF_0(1+g)}{k-g}$

In our case:

$PV = \dfrac{\$200(1+0.05)}{0.15-0.05}$

$\quad = \dfrac{\$200 \times 1.05}{0.10}$

$\quad = \$2,100$

15. $PV = \dfrac{NCF_1}{(1+k)} + \dfrac{NCF_2}{(1+k)^2} + \ldots \dfrac{NCF_n}{(1+k)^n} + \dfrac{\dfrac{NCF_n(1+g)}{k-g}}{(1+k)^n}$

In our case:

$PV = \dfrac{\$150}{(1+0.10)} + \dfrac{\$250}{(1+0.10)^2} + \dfrac{\$350}{(1+0.10)^3} + \dfrac{\dfrac{\$350(1+0.05)}{0.10-0.05}}{(1+0.10)^3}$

$\quad = \$136.36 \; + \; \$206.61 \; + \; \$262.96 \; + \; \dfrac{\dfrac{\$367.50}{0.05}}{1.33}$

$\quad = \$136.36 \; + \; \$206.61 \; + \; \$262.96 \; + \; \$5,522.16$

$\quad = \$6,128.09$

The estimated fair market value for the investment is \$6,128.09, and we have the opportunity to invest for \$6,000, so this would be a profitable investment.

16. The terminal (residual) value can be estimated using the formula:

$TV = \dfrac{NCF_n(1+g)}{k-g}$

In our case:

$TV = \dfrac{NCF_3(1+g)}{k-g}$

$\quad = \dfrac{\$350(1+0.05)}{0.10-0.05}$

$\quad = \$7,350$

17. To compute the present value of the terminal value, we use the following formula:

$$PV = \frac{\dfrac{NCF_n(1 + g)}{k - g}}{(1 + k)^n}$$

In our case:

$$PV = \frac{\dfrac{NCF_3(1 + g)}{k - g}}{(1 + k)^3}$$

$$\frac{\dfrac{\$7,350}{}}{(1 + 0.10)^3}$$

$$= \$5,522.16$$

18. $$PV = \frac{NCF_1}{(1 + k)^{0.5}} + \frac{NCF_2}{(1 + k)^{1.5}} + \cdots \frac{NCF_n}{(1 + k)^{n-0.5}} + \frac{\dfrac{NCF_n(1 + g)}{k - g}}{(1 + k)^{n-0.5}}$$

In our case:

$$PV = \frac{\$150}{(1 + 0.1)^{0.5}} + \frac{\$250}{(1 + 0.1)^{1.5}} + \frac{\$350}{(1 + 0.1)^{2.5}} + \frac{\dfrac{\$350(1 + 0.05)}{0.10 - 0.05}}{(1 + 0.1)^{2.5}}$$

$$= \frac{\$150}{1.05} + \frac{\$250}{1.15} + \frac{\$350}{1.27} + \frac{\$7,350}{1.27}$$

$$= \$143.02 + \$216.69 + \$275.79 + \$5,791.69$$

$$= \$6,427.19$$

Since the fair market value of the expected future stream of cash flows is higher than their price today, this would be a profitable investment.

19. $$PV = \frac{NCF_0(1 + g)}{k - g}$$

$$= \frac{\$1,000(1 + 0.05)}{0.15 - 0.05}$$

$$= \$10,500$$

Yes, investing for a price of $10,000 today would be profitable.

20. $$PV = \frac{NCF_0(1 + g)(1 + k)^{0.5}}{k - g}$$

$$= \frac{\$1,000(1 + 0.05)(1 + 0.10)^{0.5}}{0.15 - 0.05}$$

$$= \$11,012.49$$

Yes.

Chapter 11

Market Approach: Guideline Public Company Method

ANSWERS

Multiple Choice Questions

1. b. Net income is a financial variable underlying equity rather than invested capital. MVIC/sales is better than stock price/sales because it takes *all* of the invested capital to support the sales, not just the equity.

2. d. Almost no public companies have five years ahead average projected earnings available.

3. c

4. a. When valuing controlling interests, lean toward invested capital multiples because the control owner has the ability to change the capital structure.

5. c. Public company transactions are, by definition, marketable minorities. The price, however, may be at, or even above, control value.

True or False Questions

6. True.

7. False. Thousands of limited partnerships are registered with the SEC, and a few hundred of them have a limited trading market. Data on 100 or more with a limited trading market is published by Partnership Profiles, Inc., so it is possible to use the guideline public company method for family limited partnerships.

8. True.

9. True.

10. True.

Fill-in-the-Blank Questions

11. Electronic Data Gathering, Analysis, and Retrieval (It is the SEC's system for gathering public company data and making it available to the public.)

12. An annual report filed in accordance with SEC regulations

13. A quarterly report filed in accordance with SEC requirements

14. 8-K

15. Standard Industrial Classification (Last updated in 1987. The North American Industry Classification System [NAICS] is expected to supersede the SIC system.)

Chapter 12

Market Approach: Guideline Merger and Acquisition Method

ANSWERS

Multiple Choice Questions

1. b
2. c
3. d
4. b
5. a
6. a
7. d
8. b
9. b

True or False Questions

10. True.

11. True. The public companies had oversight by boards of directors, most of which appointed an independent committee to investigate the fairness of the proposed transaction.

    Almost all the private companies in the database were sold through intermediaries (business brokers, merger and acquisition specialists, and investment bankers), because the intermediaries are the primary sources of information for the private company transaction databases.

12. True.

Fill-in-the-Blank Questions

13. The *IBA Market Database*. Going back over 20 years, it has over 23,000 transactions—by far the most of any database.

14. *Pratt's Stats*™. It has up to 80 data points per transaction—far more than any other of the databases.

Chapter 13

Prior Transactions, Offers, and Buy-Sell Agreements

ANSWERS

True or False Questions

1. True, but even a transaction between related parties, if negotiated, may provide evidence of value.

2. True. This is often an overlooked category of prior transactions that may provide some of the best evidence of value.

3. False. It is possible that an estate could be liable for more dollars of estate tax than it would receive on a sale forced by a buy-sell agreement.

Fill-In-the-Blank Questions

4. • Internal company conditions: e.g., earnings, cash flow, asset values, qualitative conditions such as management changes

   • External market conditions: e.g., changes in stock price indexes for the industry, competitive conditions in the markets for the company's products

5. • Was the offer bona fide?

   • Was it on an arm's-length basis?

   • Did the offeror have the financial means to consummate the transaction?

   • Is enough information available to calculate valuation multiples and a cash-equivalent price?

6. • Was the buy-sell agreement negotiated and executed at arm's length?

   • Is it enforceable?

   • Has it been applied in past transactions?

   • Does it govern the transaction for which the valuation is being performed?

   • How does it affect marketability? Does it provide liquidity? Does it restrict marketability?

   • Was it representative of what rational unrelated parties, acting in their self-interests, could have agreed to at the time?

Chapter 14

Adjusted Net Asset Method

ANSWERS

Multiple Choice Questions

1. d. In such a situation, it is unlikely that an asset approach would contribute anything to the valuation. The analyst probably would rely on the market approach and/or the income approach.

2. a. The income approach is used most often to value intangible assets, partly because it addresses directly what creates value in the intangible and partly because of difficulty in obtaining reliable data for other approaches.

3. a

4. b

True or False Questions

5. True.

6. True.

7. False. Since the *Davis* case in 1998, the U.S. Tax Court has consistently recognized a discount for a C corporation holding highly appreciated stock or other saleable assets such as timber.

8. True.

Fill-in-the-Blank Questions

9. a. Going concern

   b. Liquidation

10. a. Yield capitalization method

    b. Direct capitalization method

Chapter 15

Excess Earnings Method

ANSWERS

Multiple Choice Questions

1. a. It was promulgated as Appeals and Review Memorandum 34 (ARM 34) to determine the amount of compensation that the U.S. government should pay to brewers and distillers for their goodwill lost as a result of Prohibition.

2. b

3. b. It is used and accepted most widely in family law courts, but other methods (e.g., discounted cash flow) are gaining ground.

True or False Questions

4. True.

5. False. There are so many ambiguities in the relevant Revenue Ruling that the implementation of the excess earnings method is highly inconsistent.

6. False. The ruling states that the 8 to 10% and 15 to 20% ranges are "used as examples" and that the percentage of return "should be the percentage prevailing in the industry involved at the date of valuation."

7. True.

8. False. RR 68-609 states, "If the business is a sole proprietorship or partnership, there should be deducted from the earnings of the business a reasonable amount for the services performed by the owner or partners engaged in the business."

9. False. RR 68-609 states, "The 'formula' approach may be used in determining the fair market value of intangible assets of a business only if there is no better basis available for making the determination. ...The 'formula' approach should not be used if there is better evidence available from which the value of intangibles can be determined."

Exercises

10. Net tangible asset value		$100,000
Required return on tangible assets:	$0.08 \times \$100,000 =$	$8,000
Excess earnings:	$\$40,000 - \$8,000 =$	$32,000
Value of excess earnings capitalized at 16%:	$\$32,000 / 0.16 =$	$200,000
Total value of company by excess earnings method:		$300,000

11. The WACC is computed by dividing the normalized income by the indicated value of the company.

    In our case, $\dfrac{\$40,000}{\$300,000}$ = 0.133 = 13.3%

12. Unless this is a very low-risk, high-growth business, $300,000 is a very high price for it. A 13.3% WACC is very low. The capitalization rates for both tangible assets and excess earnings are unreasonably low. Few banks will loan at 8% on tangible assets, nor will they loan 100% of tangible assets, so the rate of return on tangible assets should be a blend of cost of debt and cost of equity. At 16% and the present income level, it would take over six years of excess earnings to just recover the investment, much less to make a return on it.

Chapter 16

Discounts and Premiums

ANSWERS

Multiple Choice Questions

1. c. But while, by definition, it is marketable minority, the value may be at or above every control value, depending on the market.

2. a. The *Mergerstat/Shannon Pratt's Control Premium Study*™ showed that, for the 16 quarters of 1998 through 2001, 16% of domestic takeovers occurred at prices below their previous market trading prices and 19% of foreign takeovers were at less than their previous public market prices.

3. c

4. c. The implied minority discount can be calculated as:

   $1 - [1 \div (1 + \text{premium paid})]$

   For example, if a 25% premium were paid:

   $1 - [1 \div (1 + 25\%)]$

   $= 1 - 1 / 1.25$

   $= 1 - 0.80$

   $= 0.20 \text{ or } 20\%$

   Of course, the premium paid in transactions may include synergies, but the database transactions are coded as follows to assist the analyst in sorting out synergistic transactions:

   H—Horizontal integration

   V—Vertical integration

   C—Conglomerate

   F—Financial

5. c

6. b. As of late 2002, *The FMV Restricted Stock Study*™ had 243 transactions with 34 items of information per transaction.

7. c

8. b

True or False Questions

9. True.

10. True.

11. True.

12. False. Only control stockholders can register stock for a public offering because it requires filings by the company with the SEC.

Fill-in-the-Blank Questions

13. Portfolio (sometimes also called a discount for nonhomogeneous assets)

14. Blockage (sometimes also called an absorption discount)

Exercise

15. Control value: $12.00
    Less 20% minority discount: $0.20 \times \$12.00 = \$2.40$
    Marketable minority value: $9.60
    Less 40% discount for lack of marketability: $0.40 \times \$9.60 = \$3.84$
    Minority nonmarketable value: $5.76

    The total discount is 52%, not 60%, because the discounts are multiplicative (taken in chain) rather than additive (although a few judges actually have applied these discounts additively).

Reconciliation and Value Conclusion

ANSWERS

Multiple Choice Questions

1. d. Holding companies usually are valued with relatively more emphasis on asset values.

2. a. Inventory plays a large part in the value of distribution companies.

True or False Questions

3. False. IRS Revenue Rulings represent the position of the Service but are not legally binding.

4. True.

5. False. A high coefficient of variation among the multiples means a high degree of dispersion. Most weight should be accorded the multiples with the *least* dispersion (most tightly clustered), because those are indicative of what the market pays most attention to in the given industry.

PART IV
Analysis of the Company

Chapter 18

Financial Statement Analysis

ANSWERS

Multiple Choice Questions

1. b. III is incorrect; book values are typically used.
2. d. I is a leverage ratio. III is a liquidity ratio.
3. a. IV is an activity ratio. V is a liquidity ratio.
4. d. I and V are both leverage ratios.
5. d
6. b. I and II are both nonrecurring item adjustments.

True or False Questions

7. True.
8. True.

Exercises

9. Inventory turnover $= \dfrac{\text{Cost of goods sold}}{\text{Inventory}}$

$= \dfrac{\$7,946,744}{\$4,129,524}$

$= 1.9$

10. Return on investment $= \dfrac{\text{net income} + [(\text{interest})(1 - \text{tax rate})]}{\text{equity} + \text{long-term debt}}$

$= \dfrac{\$1,042,881 + [\$261,212(1 - 0.237)]}{\$6,319,520 + \$1,341,012}$

$= 16.2\%$

11. Current ratio $= \dfrac{\text{current assets}}{\text{current liabilities}}$

$= \dfrac{\$7,637,966}{\$4,051,227}$

$= 1.9$

12. Quick ratio $=$ $\dfrac{\text{cash} + \text{short-term investments (cash equivalents)} + \text{accounts receivable}}{\text{current liabilities}}$

$= \dfrac{\$59,847 + \$251,764 + \$3,196,831}{\$4,051,227}$

$= 0.9$

13. Times interest earned $= \dfrac{\text{EBIT}}{\text{Interest expense}}$

$= \dfrac{\$1,627,386}{\$261,212}$

$= 6.2$

Using Economic and Industry Data

ANSWERS

Multiple Choice Questions

1. a
2. c
3. b
4. c
5. a
6. d. It provides national economic information.

True or False Questions

7. False. The most frequent adjustment is for owners' compensation.
8. False. All of the statement is true except that the source of information is CPA firms, not tax returns.
9. True.

Chapter 20

Site Visits and Interviews

ANSWERS

Multiple Choice Question

1. b. Statement II is not a general objective.

True or False Questions

2. False. The analyst is valuing returns only to the *current* level of investment.
3. False. It is best to do it before the interview so you will have some questions for clarification.
4. True.

Fill-in-the-Blank Questions

5. Possible answers:
   - Layout and flow of products
   - Physical efficiency of operation
   - Cleanliness
   - Age of equipment
   - Capacity constraints
   - Environmental problems
6. Possible answers:
   - Facilities
   - Operations
   - Physical efficiency
   - Cleanliness
   - Age of equipment
   - Capacity constraints
   - Environmental problems
   - Philosophy of management
   - Quality of management
   - Company outlook
   - Strengths, weaknesses, opportunities, and threats
   - Historical trends
   - Sales growth assessment
   - Net income or net cash flow growth assessment

PART V
Supporting Data

Chapter 21

Sources of Supporting Data

ANSWERS

Multiple Choice Questions

1. d
2. c
3. d
4. b
5. a
6. d
7. d
8. b

True or False Questions

9. False. *Pratt's Stats*™ is a source of data for merged and acquired private companies.

10. False. There are multiple differences between the two series—one of them is that while the *Mergerstat/Shannon Pratt's Control Premium Study*™ focuses more on in-depth transactions, *Mergerstat*® *Review* focuses more on aggregate averages and trends. For more differences, see *"Mergerstat/Shannon Pratt's Control Premium Study*™ and *Mergerstat*® *Review Are Two Distinct Services,"* by Shannon Pratt, *Shannon Pratt's Business Valuation Update*® (April 2002):1, 5–6.

11. False. Currently there are distinct sources for public and private company data.

12. False. Determining reasonable compensation levels is an important part of a valuation engagement. Appraisers must consult sources of compensation data to find the "market levels" in order to determine reasonable compensation.

13. True.

14. True.

Fill-in-the-Blank Questions

15. Discounts for lack of marketability (based on restricted stock transactions)

16. Pre-IPO; discounts for lack of marketability

17. Outlook

PART VI
Valuations for Specific Purposes

Chapter 22

Tax-Related Valuations

ANSWERS

Multiple Choice Questions

1. a

2. b. Although it is not listed as one of the "basic eight," whether the company is dependent on a key person is a factor to consider. It can affect the discount rate in the income approach or the multiples in the market approach, or it may even be the basis for a separate discount.

3. c

4. a. Although not required in the regulations, courts certainly recognize professional certifications when qualifying and evaluating expert witnesses.

True or False Questions

5. True.

6. True.

7. True. This is one of the reasons, when valuing a family limited partnership (FLP) interest or limited liability company (LLC) interest, the analyst should:

   a. Know the state in which the entity is registered.

   b. Read the articles of partnership or other controlling documents.

   c. Read the applicable state laws.

   d. Get a representation from the client's attorney as to the interpretation of the state laws and their effect on the entity.

8. True. In one U.S. Tax Court case, a deduction for a substantial charitable contribution was disallowed for failure to comply with this requirement, even though the Service agreed that the amount claimed represented fair market value for the property.

Chapter 23

Employee Stock Ownership Plans

ANSWERS

Multiple Choice Questions

1. a. The put option must be to the company, not to the ESOP. The ESOP can have the right, but not the obligation, to buy stock from retiring employees who wish to sell.

2. c. Because of these features, many companies establish a separate class of dividend-paying stock just for the ESOP.

3. c

True or False Questions

4. False. The majority of ESOP valuations are done on a minority basis, including some in which the ESOP actually does have control, even 100% control.

5. False. The proposed DOL regulations define *fair market value* the same as the Treasury regulations.

6. True.

7. False. The appraiser is a financial advisor to the ESOP fiduciary but not a fiduciary himself or herself.

8. True.

9. True.

Fill-in-the-Blank Questions

10. Employee Retirement Income Security Act (passed in 1974)

11. Possible answers:

    - Internal Revenue Service (IRS)
    - Department of Labor (DOL)
    - Plan participants
    - Spouses of plan participants
    - Beneficiaries of plan participants

12. Repurchase liability

Chapter 24

Shareholder Buyouts and Disputes

ANSWERS

Multiple Choice Questions

1. d. Some states have case law that disallows either, and the trend is in that direction. However, far fewer than a majority of states have case law disallowing either. Some allow minority but not marketability discounts. Some allow marketability but not minority discounts. Some allow both. Some have case law stating that the issue will be decided on a case-by-case basis. Some have no precedential case law on the issue.

2. d

3. a. But all the methods listed are recognized and accepted, as is the asset approach (although the asset approach seldom is used because the premise of value usually is going concern). When the guideline public company method is used, a control premium often is applied because this method is based on transactions in minority interests.

4. b

5. a

6. d

True or False Questions

7. True.

8. True.

9. True.

Fill-in-the-Blank Questions

10. The Delaware Block Method. Until the *Weinberger v. UOP* case in 1983, Delaware dissenting stockholder cases usually were decided by applying a percentage weight to each of several factors, such as market value, asset value, and earnings value. In 1983 the *Weinberger* case, which was decided at the Court of Chancery level on the basis of the traditional Delaware Block Method, was remanded by the Delaware Supreme Court because projections that existed for the selling company (discounted cash flow method) were not considered. The *Weinberger* case stated that *all* relevant factors must be considered.

11. Going concern; liquidation

Chapter 25

Marital Dissolutions

ANSWERS

Multiple Choice Questions

1. d

2. d

3. d. But family law courts often follow the U.S. Tax Court. Does it seem fair to distribute free and clear assets to one spouse and to distribute to the other spouse assets of the same value that will be subject to a capital gains tax liability when they are sold?

True or False Questions

4. True.

5. False. A few states follow fair market value fairly closely, but most do not. Even where the phrase *fair market value* is found in an opinion, the analyst should not conclude automatically that the fair market value standard as interpreted by the Tax Court is followed; elements of what we know as "investment value" (value to a particular owner) often are reflected.

6. False. Family law courts have wide discretion in setting the valuation date. It could be the date of trial, date of separation, date of filing, or some other date.

7. False. Family law courts are extremely inconsistent about the issues of minority status and lack of marketability.

8. True, but sometimes it is difficult to convince lawyers to enforce this right.

CPE Self-Study
Examination

Business Valuation Body of Knowledge

Second Edition

Workbook

CPE SELF-STUDY EXAMINATION

About the CPE Self-Study Examination

Prerequisites: None
Recommended CPE credits: 8 Hours
Knowledge level: Basic
Area of study: Management/Consulting Services

The credit hours are in accordance with the AICPA Standards for CPE programs. Since CPE requirements are set by each state, you need to check with your State Board of Accountancy concerning required CPE hours and fields of study.

If you decide to take this CPE examination, follow the directions below. This examination fee is $59.00. Means of payment are shown on the answer form.

The CPE examination is graded no later than 2 weeks after receipt. The passing score is at least 70%. John Wiley & Sons, Inc. will issue a certificate of completion to successful participants to recognize their achievement.[*]

Photocopy one copy of the answer sheet for each additional participant who wishes to take the CPE examination. Each participant should complete the answer form and return it with the $59 fee.

The enclosed CPE examination will expire on January 1, 2006. Completed exams must be postmarked by that date.

Directions for the CPE Course:

Complete the examination after reading all chapters in *Business Valuation Body of Knowledge Workbook, Second Edition*. Record your answers by writing a letter (a–e), true, or false on the line for that question on the answer form. Upon completion of the examination, cut out the answer sheet, enclose it in a stamped envelope, and mail to the following address:

CPE Director
John Wiley & Sons, Inc.
7222 Commerce Center Drive, Suite 240
Colorado Springs, CO 80919

---

[*] Registered with the National Association of State Boards of Accountancy as a sponsor of continuity professional education on the National Registry of CPE Sponsors. State boards of accountancy have final authority on the acceptance of individual courses. Complaints regarding registered sponsors may be addressed to NASBA, 150 Fourth Avenue North, Ste. 700, Nashville, TN 37219-2417, (615) 880-4200, (615) 880-4292 (Fax).

BUSINESS VALUATION BODY OF KNOWLEDGE, *Second Edition* WORKBOOK

CPE Examination

Record your CPE answers on the answer form provided below and return this page for grading.

Mail to:

CPE Director

John Wiley & Sons, Inc., 7222 Commerce Center Drive, Suite 240, Colorado Springs, CO 80919

PAYMENT OPTIONS

☐ **Payment enclosed ($59.00).**
(Make checks payable to John Wiley & Sons, Inc.)
Please add appropriate sales tax.
Be sure to sign your order below.

Charge my:
☐ American Express
☐ Master Card
☐ Visa

Account number _____

Expiration date _____
Please sign below for all credit card orders.

Signature _____

NAME _____

FIRM NAME _____

ADDRESS _____

_____

PHONE (   ) _____

CPA STATE LICENSE # _____

CPE ANSWERS

1. ____ 2. ____ 3. ____ 4. ____ 5. ____ 6. ____ 7. ____ 8. ____ 9. ____ 10. ____
11. ____ 12. ____ 13. ____ 14. ____ 15. ____ 16. ____ 17. ____ 18. ____ 19. ____ 20. ____
21. ____ 22. ____ 23. ____ 24. ____ 25. ____ 26. ____ 27. ____ 28. ____ 29. ____ 30. ____
31. ____ 32. ____ 33. ____ 34. ____ 35. ____ 36. ____ 37. ____ 38. ____ 39. ____ 40. ____

CPE Exam ISBN: 0-471-42758-6

BUSINESS VALUATION BODY OF KNOWLEDGE, *Second Edition* WORKBOOK

CPE Feedback

1. Do you agree with the publisher's determination of CPE credit hours? Yes ____ No ____
2. Was the content relevant?   Yes ____ No ____
3. Was the content displayed clearly?   Yes ____ No ____
4. Did the content enhance your professional competence?   Yes ____ No ____
5. Was the content timely and effective?   Yes ____ No ____

How can we make the examination/content better? If you have any suggestions, please summarize them in the space below. We will consider them in developing future examinations.

_____

_____

_____

_____

_____

_____

_____

_____

_____

CPE Self-Study Examination

MULTIPLE CHOICE QUESTIONS

1. Which of the following are governed by federal rather than state law?

   a. Minority oppression actions

   b. Bankruptcy reorganizations

   c. Eminent domain proceedings

   d. Dissenting stockholder suits

2. What is the number of the Revenue Ruling that relates to discounts for lack of marketability?

   a. 59-60

   b. 68-609

   c. 77-287

   d. 93-12

3. The *Uniform Standards of Professional Appraisal Practice (USPAP)* is published by which of the following organizations?

   a. American Institute of Certified Public Accountants (AICPA)

   b. American Society of Appraisers (ASA)

   c. The Appraisal Foundation

   d. National Association of Certified Valuation Analysts (NACVA)

4. Which of the following organizations issues the credential Accredited Member (AM)?

   a. National Association of Certified Valuation Analysts (NACVA)

   b. Institute of Business Appraisers (IBA)

   c. American Society of Appraisers (ASA)

   d. Canadian Institute of Chartered Business Valuators (CICBV)

5. Most state statutes have the standard of *fair value* for which of the following?

   a. Dissenting stockholder suits, minority oppression suits, and marital dissolutions

   b. Dissenting stockholder suits and marital dissolutions

   c. Minority oppression suits and marital dissolutions

   d. Dissenting stockholder suits and minority oppression suits

6. Alternative dispute resolution can include which of the following options?

   a. Binding and nonbinding arbitration and binding or nonbinding mediation

   b. Binding or nonbinding arbitration and nonbinding mediation

   c. Binding arbitration and nonbinding mediation

   d. Nonbinding arbitration and nonbinding mediation

7. In the hierarchy of business appraisal nomenclature, what is the term that usually is applied to the *broadest* category of methodology?

   a. Approach

   b. Method

   c. Procedure

   d. Technique

8. The subscript $_1$ usually refers to what period or periods?

   a. The period immediately prior to the valuation date

   b. The period immediately following the valuation date

   c. 19×1 or 20×1 in the numbering of the historical or forecasted results

   d. The average for some number of years beginning with year 1

9. In the notation of the weighted average cost of capital (WACC), what is the notation W_e generally understood to stand for?

   a. The weight of common equity at book value

   b. The combined weight of common and preferred equity at book value

   c. The weight of common equity at market value

   d. The combined weight of common and preferred equity at market value

10. Which of the following is the statutory standard of value for marital dissolutions in most states?

    a. Fair market value

    b. Fair value

    c. Intrinsic value

    d. None

11. What is the *best* answer for what is included in *invested capital*?

    a. Accounts payable, long-term debt, preferred equity, and common equity

    b. Long-term debt, preferred equity, and common equity

    c. Preferred and common equity

    d. Common equity only

12. For a company with 50% debt, 50% equity, and a 50% tax rate, the relationship between the levered and unlevered beta can be summarized as:

    a. Beta levered is one and a half beta unlevered.

    b. Beta levered is half beta unlevered.

    c. Beta unlevered is one and a half beta levered.

    d. Beta unlevered is half beta levered.

13. The single most important reason why different companies have different costs of capital is because:

    a. Companies differ in terms of the amounts of cash available to be distributed in the form of dividends and interest to their investors.

    b. Companies have different capital structures that cause the different components of the capital structure to be weighted differently.

    c. Companies differ in terms of their expense structures.

    d. Companies differ in terms of the expected rate of sales growth in perpetuity.

14. The following are known about Company ABC (capital structure percentages based on market prices):

Percentage of debt in capital structure:	25%
Percentage of preferred equity in capital structure:	25%
Percentage of common equity in capital structure:	50%
Cost of debt pretax:	10%
Tax rate:	40%
Cost of preferred equity:	16%
Beta:	2
Risk-free rate:	6%
General risk premium:	7%

The after-tax cost of debt, cost of equity capital, and the WACC, respectively, for Company ABC are:

a. 6%, 19%, and 15%

b. 6%, 20%, and 15.5%

c. 4%, 19%, and 14.5%

d. 4%, 20%, and 15%

15. All of the following statements about cost of capital are true EXCEPT:

a. Cost of capital is a function of the investment, not the investor.

b. Cost of capital usually is stated in real terms.

c. Cost of capital is based on expected returns relative to market prices.

d. The basic components of cost of capital are the risk-free rate and a risk premium.

16. An investment is expected to yield $100, $150, $200, and $1,000 in years 1, 2, 3, and 4, respectively. The cost of capital applicable to the stream of expected cash flows is 10%. The value of the investment under the year-end and midyear conventions, respectively, is closest to:

a. $1,097.44 (year-end) and $1,050.19 (midyear)

b. $1,050.19 (year-end) and $1,097.44 (midyear)

c. $1,097.44 (year-end) and $1,097.44 (midyear)

d. $1,050.19 (year-end) and $1,050.19 (midyear)

17. Which of the following is the correct formula for the capitalization model known as the Gordon Growth Model?

   a. $PV = NCF_0 (1 + g) / (g - k)$

   b. $PV = NCF_0 / (g - k) (1 + g)$

   c. $PV = NCF_0 (1 + g) / (k - g)$

   d. $PV = NCF_0 / (k - g) (1 + g)$

18. The following are known about an investment:

   • Expected cash flows at the end of years 1, 2, and 3 are $100, $150, and $200, respectively.

   • After year 3, cash flow is expected to increase at a steady rate of 5% in perpetuity.

   • The cost of capital for the investment is estimated to be 10%.

   The present value of the terminal or residual value under the year-end and the midyear conventions, respectively, is closest to:

   a. $2,876.71 (year-end) and $3,000 (midyear)

   b. $2,876.71 (year-end) and $3,307.09 (midyear)

   c. $3,157.89 (year-end) and $3,307.09 (midyear)

   d. $3,000 (year-end) and $3,157.89 (midyear)

19. Which of the following is a correct statement about relative analysis of the subject company versus guideline companies?

   a. If the subject company has higher growth prospects, that would lead to a higher capitalization rate in the income approach.

   b. If the subject company has higher growth prospects, that would lead to higher valuation multiples in the market approach.

   c. If the subject company has a higher risk profile, that would lead to a lower capitalization rate in the income approach.

   d. If the subject company has a higher risk profile, that would lead to higher valuation multiples in the market approach.

20. What is an 8-K?

    a. An annual report filed with the SEC

    b. A quarterly report filed with the SEC

    c. A significant special events report filed with the SEC

    d. A "small business" report (under $25 million market capitalization of equity) filed with the SEC

21. Which of the following company transaction databases contains the greatest amount of company information for each transaction?

    a. *Mergerstat/Shannon Pratt's Control Premium Study*™

    b. *Done Deals*®

    c. *Pratt's Stats*™

    d. *BIZCOMPS*®

22. All of the following are situations suggesting use of the adjusted net asset method EXCEPT:

    a. Company value primarily or heavily depends on asset values, such as a holding company.

    b. Highly profitable high-tech company has assets fully depreciated on its books.

    c. Purchase price allocations are required.

    d. Nonoperating assets are a factor.

23. What is the number of the "excess earnings" Revenue Ruling?

    a. 93-12

    b. 83-120

    c. 77-287

    d. 68-609

24. Which of the following is a pre-IPO transaction study for discounts for lack of marketability rather than a restricted stock study?

    a. SEC Institutional Investor Study

    b. Moroney Study

    c. Valuation Advisors Study

    d. FMV Opinions Study

25. For which of the following broad industry groups are asset values usually accorded the most weight?

    a. Manufacturing companies

    b. Financial institutions

    c. Service companies

    d. Professional practices

26. In financial statement analysis, which of the following is considered an *activity* ratio?

    a. Inventory turnover

    b. Current ratio

    c. Quick ratio

    d. Equity to total capital

27. All of the following are sources of industry outlook information EXCEPT:

    a. *First Industry Research Profiles*

    b. *Almanac of Business and Industrial Financial Ratios*

    c. *U.S. Industry and Trade Outlook*

    d. *Standard & Poor's Industry Surveys*

28. Which of the following is based on tax return data?

    a. *Almanac of Business and Industrial Financial Ratios*

    b. Risk Management Association's (formerly Robert Morris Associates) *Annual Statement Studies*

    c. Financial Research Association's *Financial Studies of the Small Business*

    d. Ibbotson's *Cost of Capital Yearbook*

29. If a site visit and management interview are to be conducted in conjunction with a business valuation, when is generally the optimal time to do it?

    a. At the outset of the engagement

    b. When the analyst first receives documents relating to the engagement

    c. After the analyst has received and done some analysis of the documents

    d. As the final step of the engagement

30. When valuing a small private company and looking for comparable merged or acquired companies, which of the following sources of data would be the LEAST helpful?

    a. *BIZCOMPS®*

    b. *EDGAR*

    c. *Pratt's Stats*™

    d. *IBA Market Database*

31. According to Revenue Ruling 66-49, which applies to appraisals of charitable contributions of noncash property for federal income tax purposes, what is the maximum amount of time before the date of the contribution that the appraisal may be done without being outdated?

    a. 30 days

    b. 60 days

    c. 90 days

    d. 120 days

32. What is the essence of the Delaware Block Method?

   a. The size of the block of stock must be considered when deciding whether, or how much, blockage discount should be applied.

   b. All relevant factors must be considered when valuing a block of stock.

   c. The conclusion of value is reached by applying percentage weights to the values indicated by each of several factors, such as market value, asset value, and earnings value.

   d. The market approach should be accorded no more than a proportionate share of the weight.

33. What is the statutory standard of value for dissenting stockholder actions in most states?

   a. Fair market value

   b. Fair value

   c. Intrinsic value

   d. None

TRUE OR FALSE QUESTIONS

34. For estate tax purposes, the effective valuation date must be either the date of death or the alternative valuation date, which is six months after death. True False

35. Interrogatories are questions that the plaintiff or defendant can ask of the opposing party and that must be answered in writing and under oath. True False

36. "Midyear discounting" is a convention used in the discounted future earnings (discounted cash flow) method that reflects economic benefits being generated at midyear, approximately the effect of economic benefits being generated evenly throughout the year. True False

37. In the capitalization method, all changes in the expected future increments of return are captured in the numerator, while in the discounting method they are captured in the denominator. True False

38. In analyzing financial statements for the market approach, nonrecurring items should be adjusted out of both the subject company statements and the guideline company statements. True False

39. One category of prior transactions that is often overlooked but may provide some excellent evidence of value is acquisitions made by the subject company.   True   False

40. It is not usually necessary to do a site visit or a management interview in conjunction with a business appraisal.   True   False

Index

Index

This index has been prepared to help the reader who would like to strengthen his or her grasp of a particular aspect of the vast body of business valuation knowledge. To that end, the questions have all been indexed by topic, so a reader desiring to work through questions only on a particular subject matter can easily find the relevant questions. To avoid confusing readers, only the questions—not the answers—are indexed.

The format is simple: Entries are indexed to specific questions on particular pages. For example, an index entry followed by 31-Q4 means that the subject of that entry can be found on page 31 in question 4.

Of course, the answers should be consulted in conjunction with working through the subject questions.

10-K, 40-Q12
10-Q, 40-Q13

Accredited in Business Valuation
 (ABV), 6-Q3
Acquisition value, *see* transaction
 value
Activity ratios, 59-Q2, 61-Q7
Ad valorem (property) taxes
 Governing law, 3-Q1
 Intangible value, 10-Q8
Adjusted net asset method (asset
 accumulation method)
 Discount for lack of marketability,
  48-Q6
 Discount for minority status, 48-Q6
 Value produced by, 22-Q5, 48-Q6
 Value reconciliation, 55-Q1
*Almanac of Business and Industrial
 Financial Ratios*, 64-Q1, 64-Q2,
 73-Q8
Alternatives to litigation, 11-Q2
American Society of Appraisers (ASA),
 6-Q4, 6-Q5

American Stock Exchange (AMEX),
 17-Q2
American Institute of Certified Public
 Accountants (AICPA), 6-Q3,
 6-Q5
Annual Statement Studies, 64-Q1
Appraisal Foundation, The
 Generally, 5-Q1, 5-Q2, 7-Q9
 Appraisal Qualifications Board
  (AQB), 5-Q1
 Appraisal Standards Board (ASB),
  5-Q1, 5-Q2, 7-Q9
 Industry Advisory Council (IAC),
  5-Q1
 Requirements of business appraisal
  standards, 5-Q2
 The Appraisal Foundation Advisory
  Council (TAFAC), 5-Q1
Approach, *see* valuation approach
Arbitrage pricing model (APM), 15-Q1,
 28-Q27, 72-Q3, 72-Q6
Arbitration, 11-Q2
Arithmetic average, 27-Q19
Asset accumulation method, *see*
 adjusted net asset method

Asset appraisal
  Machinery and equipment appraisal, 47-Q3
  Real estate appraisal, 47-Q3, 48-Q10
  Situations when needed, 47-Q1
Asset liquidations, 47-Q1
Asset-based approach, *see* adjusted net asset method
Attribution, 77-Q3
Average
  Generally, 17-Q1
  Arithmetic, 27-Q19
  Geometric, 27-Q19
Association for Investment Management and Research (AIMR), 6-Q4

Baird & Co. Studies, *see* Emory Studies
Bankruptcy
  Appraisal approaches, 84-Q9
  Premise of value, 84-Q11
  Standard of value, 83-Q5
Base period, 18-Q3
Bench trial, 12-Q4
Beta
  Generally, 16-Q3
  CAPM, 28-Q25
  Levered, 27-Q20, 29-Q37
  Private companies, 28-Q26
  Unlevered, 27-Q20, 29-Q38
BIRR Risks and Returns Analyzer®, 72-Q6
BIZCOMPS®, 41-Q1, 42-Q4, 42-Q6, 73-Q7
Block size, 52-Q3
Book value, 18-Q5
Build-up model, 15-Q1
Business Appraisal Practice (journal), 6-Q6
Business risk, 16-Q3
Business Valuation Review (journal), 6-Q5

Buyout
  Discount for lack of marketability, 52-Q3
  Minority stockholders, 84-Q7, 84-Q8
Buy-sell agreement
  Areas to investigate, 46-Q6
  Estate tax purposes, 45-Q3, 78-Q6
  Standard of value, 83-Q6

Canadian Institute of Chartered Business Valuators (CICBV), 6-Q4, 6-Q5
Capital Asset Pricing Model (CAPM)
  Generally, 15-Q1, 26-Q17
  Beta, 28-Q25
  Modified (expanded) CAPM, 27-Q18
  Size premium, 28-Q25
Capital gains, *see* discount for trapped-in capital gains
Capital structure
  Components, 23-Q2, 28-Q30
  Minority interest, 27-Q23
Capitalization method
  Generally, 34-Q2, 35-Q7, 35-Q8, 36-Q10
  Compared with real estate appraisal method, 48-Q10
  Dissenting stockholder actions, 83-Q3
  Growth, 35-Q8, 35-Q9
  Measure of economic income, 36-Q11
  No-growth methodology, 35-Q9
  Terminal value, 30-Q2
  Two-stage model, 35-Q5
  Value produced by, 35-Q3
  Versus discounting method, 34-Q1, 35-Q3
Capitalization rate
  Generally, 18-Q6
  Excess earnings method, 50-Q6, 50-Q11

Growth rate, 34-Q2, 35-Q3, 35-Q8
  Relationship with multiple, 16-Q6
  Versus discount rate, 34-Q2, 35-Q3
Cash flows
  Capitalization method, 35-Q3
  DCF method, 22-Q5, 35-Q3
  Future, 16-Q10, 35-Q6
  Probability distribution, 33-Q16
CAVS, 7-Q10
Census of Manufacturers, 73-Q14
Census of Service Industries, 73-Q14
Census of Wholesale Trade, 73-Q14
Certified Business Appraiser (CBA),
  6-Q3
Certified Valuation Analyst (CVA),
  6-Q3
Charitable contributions
  Appraisal summary requirements,
    78-Q8
  Qualified appraiser requirements,
    78-Q4
Chartered Business Valuator (CBV),
  6-Q3
Chartered Financial Analyst (CFA),
  6-Q4
Coefficient of variation
  Calculated, 60-Q5
  Multiples, 39-Q4, 56-Q5
Columbia Financial Advisors Study,
  52-Q4
Compact DISEC, 72-Q5
Compensation data, 73-Q12, 66-Q9
*Complete Economic and Demographic
  Data Source*, 65-Q6
Composite data, 64-Q1, 65-Q3
COMPUSTAT, 71-Q1, 72-Q5
Control adjustments, 61-Q6, 66-Q7
Control premiums
  Data, 72-Q3
  *Mergerstat/Shannon Pratt's Control
    Premium Study*™, 41-Q2
  Negative, 51-Q2

Control value
  Adjusted net asset method, 22-Q5,
    48-Q6
  DCF method, 22-Q5
  Discounted economic income
    method, 31-Q9
  ESOPs, 80-Q4
  Excess earnings method, 22-Q5,
    50-Q4
  Guideline merger and acquisition
    method, 22-Q5
  Guideline public company method,
    39-Q5, 51-Q1
  Versus minority value, 22-Q5
Controlling interests
  Buyouts of minority stockholders,
    84-Q7, 84-Q8
  Discount for lack of marketability,
    31-Q10, 54-Q15
  Multiples, 39-Q4
Corporation Source Book, 64-Q2
Corporate dissolutions, 3-Q1
Cost approach, 47-Q2
Cost of capital
  Generally, 23-Q1, 23-Q2, 24-Q7
  Components, 23-Q3
  Discount rate, 27-Q22
  Expected rate of return, 27-Q22
  Hyperinflation, 24-Q8
  Resulting value, 24-Q5
  Subsidiary, 24-Q6
Cost of Capital Center Web site,
  71-Q1
Cost of capital data, 71-Q1, 71-Q2,
  72-Q3, 72-Q4
Cost of Capital Yearbook, 71-Q1
Cost of equity
  Generally, 25-Q11, 28-Q31
  Estimating, 15-Q1, 27-Q19, 29-Q36
  Discount rate, 32-Q12
  Pretax, 25-Q13
  WACC, 25-Q12

Cost of debt
    Generally, 23-Q2, 25-Q11
    After-tax, 25-Q9, 25-Q13, 26-Q14,
        28-Q34
    Hidden costs, 25-Q10
    Pretax, 25-Q9, 25-Q13, 26-Q14
    WACC, 25-Q12
Cost of preferred equity
    Generally, 25-Q11
    Pretax, 25-Q13
    WACC, 25-Q12
Current ratio, 62-Q11

Data sources
    Arbitrage pricing theory data, 72-Q3
    Compensation data, 66-Q9, 73-Q12
    Cost of capital data, 71-Q1, 71-Q2,
        72-Q3, 72-Q4,
    Discount and premium data, 72-Q3
    Earnings forecasts, 71-Q2, 72-Q4,
        72-Q6
    Economic data, 65-Q4, 65-Q5,
        65-Q6, 73-Q13, 73-Q14
    Guideline merger and acquisition
        data, 22-Q4, 43-Q10, 71-Q2,
        72-Q3, 72-Q4, 73-Q7
    Guideline public company data, 22-Q4,
        71-Q2, 72-Q4, 72-Q5, 73-Q9
    Industry composite data, 64-Q1, 65-Q3
    Performance data, 73-Q8
    Tax return data, 64-Q2, 65-Q3, 66-Q8
Databases
    Arm's-length transactions, 43-Q11
    BIZCOMPS®, 41-Q1, 42-Q4, 42-Q6,
        73-Q7
    Done Deals®, 41-Q1, 42-Q4, 73-Q7
    IBA Market Database, 42-Q4, 42-Q5,
        73-Q7
    Mergerstat/Shannon Pratt's Control
        Premium Study™, 41-Q1,
        41-Q2, 42-Q4, 43-Q8, 43-Q9,
        52-Q4, 72-Q3, 73-Q7, 73-Q10

Pratt's Stats™, 41-Q1, 43-Q7, 73-Q7,
    73-Q9
Date, *see* valuation date
Default risk, 26-Q15
Delaware Block Method, 56-Q4
Delaware case law, 8-Q1, 82-Q2, 83-Q3
Department of Labor (DOL) proposed
    regulations
    Definition of fair market value,
        80-Q5
    Lack of marketability, 80-Q6
Direct testimony, 11-Q3
Discounts, *see* individual discounts
Discount for lack of control, 54-Q15
    Adjusted net asset method, 48-Q6
    Data, 72-Q3
    Dissenting stockholder suits, 8-Q1,
        82-Q1, 82-Q2
    Guideline merger and acquisition
        method, 42-Q3
    Marital dissolutions, 86-Q7
    Study to help quantify, 52-Q4
Discount for lack of marketability
    (DLOM)
    Adjusted net asset method, 48-Q6
    Controlling interests, 31-Q10, 54-Q15
    Dissenting stockholder suits, 8-Q1,
        82-Q1, 82-Q2
    ESOPs, 53-Q11, 80-Q6
    Factors affecting magnitude, 52-Q3
    Guideline merger and acquisition
        method, 42-Q3
    Marital dissolutions, 86-Q7
    Minority interests, 31-Q10
    Pre-IPO studies, 53-Q7
    Restricted stock studies, 52-Q6, 53-Q8
Discount for loss of key person, 53-Q10
Discount for minority interest, *see*
    discount for lack of control
Discount for trapped-in capital gains
    Family law courts, 52-Q5, 86-Q3
    Tax Court recognition, 48-Q7, 52-Q5,
        86-Q3

Discount rate
  Generally, 16-Q10
  Cost of capital, 27-Q22
  Discounted economic income
      method, 31-Q6, 31-Q10, 32-Q12
  Expected rate of return, 27-Q22
  Growth rate, 34-Q2, 35-Q3
  Versus capitalization rate, 34-Q2,
      35-Q3
Discounted cash flow (DCF) model
  Generally, 15-Q1
  Dissenting stockholder actions, 83-Q3
  Marital dissolutions, 22-Q3
  Single-stage model, 29-Q39
  Value produced by, 22-Q5, 24-Q5
  Versus capitalization method, 35-Q3
Discounted economic income method
  Generally, 30-Q1, 32-Q11
  Compared with real estate appraisal
      method, 48-Q10
  Discount rate, 31-Q6, 31-Q10, 32-Q12
  Measure of economic income, 31-Q6
  Net cash flow, 31-Q5
  Value produced by, 31-Q9
  Versus capitalization method, 34-Q1,
      35-Q3
  Terminal value, 30-Q2
Dissenting stockholder actions
  Delaware case law, 8-Q1, 82-Q2,
      83-Q3
  Discount for lack of control, 8-Q1,
      82-Q1, 82-Q2
  Discount for lack of marketability,
      8-Q1, 82-Q1, 82-Q2
  Excess earnings method, 49-Q3
  Fair value, 10-Q7
  Governing law, 3-Q1
  Precedential case law, 8-Q1, 82-Q1
  Standard of value, 21-Q2
  Valuation date, 8-Q1
  Valuation methods, 83-Q3
  Valuation procedure, 84-Q10
Distribution companies, 55-Q2

Dividends
  Company's capacity to pay, 77-Q2
  Cumulative, 77-Q3
  Discount for lack of marketability,
      52-Q3
  ESOP stock, 79-Q2, 80-Q9
Done Deals®, 41-Q1, 42-Q4, 73-Q7

Earnings
  Excess earnings method, 50-Q7, 50-Q8
  Forecasts, 71-Q2, 72-Q4, 72-Q6
EBITDA, 18-Q7
Economic data
  Local data, 73-Q14
  National data, 65-Q5, 65-Q6, 73-Q13
  Regional data, 65-Q4, 65-Q6, 73-Q14
Economic Report of the President,
      65-Q5, 73-Q8
EDGAR, 39-Q8, 39-Q10, 40-Q11, 72-Q5
Effective date, see valuation date
Emory Studies, 53-Q7, 74-Q16
Employee Stock Ownership Plan
      (ESOP) Association, 6-Q8
Employee stock ownership plans
      (ESOPs)
  Generally, 79-Q1, 80-Q11
  Appraiser, 80-Q7
  Control basis, 80-Q4
  Department of Labor proposed
      regulations, 80-Q5, 80-Q6
  Discount for lack of marketability,
      53-Q11, 80-Q6
  Dividends, 79-Q2, 80-Q9
  ERISA, 80-Q10
  Fiduciary, 80-Q7
  Governing law, 3-Q1
  Put rights, 53-Q11, 79-Q1, 81-Q12
  Qualifying contributions, 79-Q1
  Standard of value, 21-Q1, 80-Q5
  Tax-deductibility, 79-Q1, 79-Q2,
      80-Q8
  Tax-free rollover, 80-Q3, 80-Q9

Engagement letter
  Contents, 10-Q12, 10-Q13
  Indemnification clause, 10-Q9
  Receipt of documents and
      information, 10-Q13
  Statement of contingent and limiting
      conditions, 10-Q10
  Use of valuation, 10-Q13
  Valuation date, 10-Q13
Entity-level taxes, 28-Q33
Equity
  Multiples, 39-Q4
  Valuation, 22-Q10, 35-Q7
Equity risk premium
  Arithmetic average, 27-Q19
  CAPM, 26-Q17
  Elements, 26-Q16
  Expanded CAPM, 27-Q18
  Formula for computing, 17-Q2
  Geometric average, 27-Q19
  Risk-free rate, 17-Q2, 27-Q24
ERISA, 80-Q10
Excess earnings method
  Generally, 49-Q1, 50-Q5, 50-Q10,
      50-Q12
  Capitalization rate, 50-Q6, 50-Q11
  Earnings, 50-Q7, 50-Q8
  Gift, estate, and income taxes, 49-Q3
  Intangible assets, 50-Q9
  IRS position, 22-Q7, 50-Q9
  Marital dissolutions, 22-Q3, 49-Q3
  Partnership/sole proprietorship,
      50-Q8
  Reasonable compensation disputes,
      49-Q3
  Revenue Ruling, 3-Q2, 49-Q2,
      50-Q6, 50-Q7, 50-Q8
  Return on tangible assets, 50-Q6
  Shareholder disputes, 49-Q3
  Value produced by, 22-Q5, 50-Q4
Expanded (modified) CAPM, 27-Q18
Expected inflation, 23-Q3, 24-Q4

Expected rate of return
  Generally, 23-Q1
  Cost of capital, 27-Q22
  Discount rate, 27-Q22
Expert witnesses
  Direct testimony, 11-Q3
  Hearsay exception, 12-Q5
  Hypothetical questions, 11-Q3
  Leading questions, 11-Q3
  Qualifications, 12-Q10
  Testimony, 12-Q9
  Written reports under FRCP, 11-Q1
Extraordinary items, 38-Q3

Family law courts, *see* marital
      dissolutions
Fair market value, 8-Q2, 9-Q3, 16-Q4,
      21-Q1, 21-Q2, 22-Q6, 24-Q5,
      42-Q, 3, 77-Q1, 80-Q5, 83-Q4,
      83-Q5, 83-Q6, 85-Q1, 86-Q5
Fair value, 8-Q2, 9-Q3, 10-Q7, 16-Q4,
      21-Q2, 24-Q5, 77-Q1, 83-Q4,
      83-Q5, 83-Q6, 85-Q1
Fairness opinion, 16-Q8
Family-controlled company, 77-Q3
Federal Reserve Banks, 73-Q13
      (another)
Federal Reserve Bulletin, 65-Q4, 65-Q5
Federal Rules of Civil Procedure, 4-Q5,
      11-Q1
Federal Rules of Evidence, 4-Q5
Federal law/court system, 3-Q1, 12-Q7
FIFO (first in, first out), 38-Q3
Financial Analysts Journal (journal),
      6-Q
Financial Ratio Analyst, 64-Q1
Financial Research Associates, 64-Q1
Financial risk, 16-Q3
Financial statements, 16-Q9, 38-Q3
Financial Studies of the Small Business,
      64-Q1, 66-Q8

The FMV Restricted Stock Study™, 52-Q6

Fundamental security analysis, 10-Q15

Fraud investigation, 10-Q11

Generally Accepted Accounting Principles (GAAP), 59-Q1

Geometric average, 27-Q19

Gift tax, *see* tax-related valuations

Goodwill

Generally, 16-Q7

Enterprise goodwill (entity/practice goodwill), 77-Q2

Marital dissolutions, 85-Q2

Personal goodwill, 85-Q2

Gordon Growth Model

Generally, 35-Q4

Two-stage model, 36-Q12

Growth rate

Capitalization method, 35-Q8

Capitalization rate, 34-Q2, 35-Q3, 35-Q8

Discount rate, 34-Q2, 35-Q3

Guideline merger and acquisition method

Compared with guideline public company method, 22-Q4, 43-Q12

Data available, 43-Q10, 71-Q2, 72-Q3, 72-Q4, 73-Q7

Dissenting stockholder actions, 83-Q3

Marketability discount, 42-Q3

Minority interest discount, 42-Q3

Transaction data, 22-Q4

Value produced by, 22-Q5, 43-Q12

Guideline public company method

Compared with guideline merger and acquisition method, 22-Q4, 43-Q12

Data sources, 71-Q2, 72-Q4, 72-Q5, 73-Q9

Dissenting stockholder actions, 83-Q3

Earnings periods, 38-Q2

Revenue Ruling, 39-Q6

Transaction data, 22-Q4

Value produced by, 39-Q5, 51-Q1

Harmonic mean, 17-Q1

Hearsay exception, 12-Q5

Horizon risk, 26-Q15

Hyperinflation, 24-Q8

Hypothetical questions, 11-Q3

IBA Market Database, 42-Q4, 42-Q5, 73-Q7

Ibbotson Associates

Cost of Capital Center Web site, 71-Q1

Cost of Capital Yearbook, 71-Q1

Earnings forecasts, 72-Q6

Entity-level taxes, 28-Q33

Financial statements, 38-Q3

Personal-level income taxes, 28-Q33

Stocks, Bonds, Bills and Inflation Yearbook, 71-Q1

I/B/E/S United States Database, 72-Q6

Income approach, 47-Q2

Indemnification clause, 10-Q9

Industry composite data, 64-Q1, 65-Q3

Industry Norms and Key Business Ratios, 73-Q8

Inflation, 23-Q3, 24-Q4

Institute of Business Appraisers (IBA), 6-Q4, 6-Q6

Intangible assets

Excess earnings method, 50-Q9

Valuation approach, 47-Q2

Intangible value

Ad valorem taxes, 10-Q8

Factor to consider, 77-Q2

Interest rate risk, 26-Q15

Internal Revenue Code
  Section 1042, 80-Q3
  Section 2701, chapter 14, 77-Q3
  Section 2703, chapter 14, 78-Q6
  Section 2704, chapter 14, 78-Q7
Internal Revenue Service
  Business valuation guidelines, 4-Q11
  Excess earnings method, 22-Q7, 50-Q9
  IRS Corporate Ratios, 64-Q2
  *IRS Valuation Training for Appeals
      Officers Coursebook*, 4-Q7
  Revenue rulings, 56-Q3
International Business Brokers
      Association (IBBA), 6-Q7
Interviews, 65-Q3, 67-Q1, 67-Q2,
      67-Q3, 68-Q6
Intrinsic value, 9-Q3, 16-Q4, 24-Q5,
      77-Q1, 83-Q4, 83-Q5, 85-Q1
Inventory, 48-Q4
  Accounting bases, 38-Q3
  Turnover, 59-Q2, 62-Q9
Invested capital
  Discount rate, 32-Q12
  Multiples, 38-Q1, 39-Q4
Investment risk, 16-Q3
Investment value, 8-Q2, 9-Q3, 16-Q4,
      24-Q5, 77-Q1, 83-Q4, 83-Q5,
      83-Q6
IRS, *see* Internal Revenue Service

Judge, 12-Q4, 12-Q6
Jury, 12-Q4

Key person
  Dependence, 77-Q2
  Discount, 53-Q10

Lack of marketability, *see* discount for
      lack of marketability
Leading questions, 11-Q3

Leverage ratios, 60-Q3, 61-Q8
Levered beta, 27-Q20, 29-Q37
Liquidation (salvage) method, 30-Q2
Liquidity ratios, 60-Q4
Local economic data, 73-Q14
Long-term debt, 22-Q10

Machinery and equipment appraisal,
      47-Q3
Management interviews, 65-Q3, 67-Q1,
      67-Q2, 67-Q3, 68-Q6
Management Planning Study, 52-Q6
Manufacturing companies
  Asset appraisal, 47-Q1
  Asset values, 55-Q2
Marital dissolutions
  Generally, 86-Q4, 86-Q8
  Discount for lack of marketability,
      86-Q7
  Discount for minority interest, 86-Q7
  Discount for trapped-in capital gains,
      52-Q5, 86-Q3
  Excess earnings method, 22-Q3, 49-Q3
  Goodwill, 85-Q2
  Standard of value, 8-Q2, 22-Q3,
      22-Q6, 85-Q1, 86-Q5
  Valuation date, 86-Q6
  Valuation methods, 22-Q3
Market approach
  Intangible assets, 47-Q2
  Value reconciliation, 55-Q1, 56-Q5
Market multiple method, 30-Q2
Marketability discount, *see* discount for
      lack of marketability
Marketable minority value, 39-Q5, 51-Q1
Maturity risk
  Expanded CAPM, 27-Q18
  Risk-free rate, 26-Q15
Mean, 17-Q1, 60-Q5
Median, 17-Q1, 60-Q5
Mediation, 11-Q2
Mergerstat® Review, 73-Q10

Mergerstat/Shannon Pratt's Control Premium Study™, 41-Q1, 41-Q2, 42-Q4, 43-Q8, 43-Q9, 52-Q4, 72-Q3, 73-Q7, 73-Q10
Metro Insights, 65-Q6
Midyear convention, 31-Q3, 33-Q17, 37-Q18, 37-Q20
Minority interest
  Buyouts, 84-Q7, 84-Q8
  Capital structure, 27-Q23
  Discount for lack of marketability, 31-Q10
  Multiples, 39-Q4
  Public offering, 53-Q12
  Voting versus nonvoting stock, 53-Q9
Minority interest discount, *see* discount for lack of control
Minority oppression actions
  Corporate dissolutions, 3-Q1
  Excess earnings method, 49-Q3
  Standard of value, 9-Q3, 83-Q4
  State statutes, 84-Q8
Minority value
  Asset accumulation method, 22-Q5
  DCF method, 22-Q5
  Discounted economic income method, 31-Q9
  Excess earnings method, 22-Q5
  Guideline merger and acquisition method, 22-Q5
  Versus control value, 22-Q5
Mode, 17-Q1, 60-Q5
Modified (expanded) CAPM, 27-Q18
Moody's, 72-Q4
Multiples, *see* valuation multiples
MVIC, 18-Q8, 38-Q1

Nasdaq Stock Market (NASDAQ), 17-Q2
National Association of Certified Valuation Analysts (NACVA), 6-Q5

National economic data, 65-Q5, 65-Q6, 73-Q13
Negative premiums, 51-Q2
Net cash flow
  Compared with net income, 31-Q7
  Discounted economic income method, 31-Q5
  To equity, 32-Q13
  To invested capital, 32-Q14
Net income, 31-Q7
New York Stock Exchange (NYSE), 17-Q2
Nominal rate of return, 23-Q3, 24-Q4
Noncash charitable contributions, *see* charitable contributions
Nonmarketable minority value, 39-Q5, 51-Q1, 54-Q15
Nonoperating assets, 47-Q1
Nonoperating income, 66-Q7
Nonrecurring items, 38-Q3, 59-Q1
Nonvoting stock, 53-Q9
Normalizing adjustments, 59-Q1
No-growth methodology, 35-Q9

Opportunity cost, 23-Q1
Over-the-counter (OTC) stocks, 17-Q2

Particular investor, value to, 10-Q14, 16-Q4
Partnerships, 39-Q7
Peerscape, 72-Q5
Performance data, 73-Q8
Personal-level income taxes, 28-Q33
Pratt's Stats™, 41-Q1, 43-Q7, 73-Q7, 73-Q9
Precedential case law, 8-Q1, 82-Q1
Preferred equity, 23-Q2
Premise of value, 15-Q2, 48-Q9, 84-Q11
Present value, 16-Q10
Pre-IPO studies, 53-Q7
Principle of substitution, 23-Q1

Prior offers, 45-Q5

Prior transactions, 45-Q1, 45-Q2, 45-Q4

Private Letter Rulings (PLRs), 4-Q6

Procedure, *see* valuation procedure

Professional practices, 55-Q2

Public offering
   Discount for lack of marketability,
      52-Q3
   Minority stockholders, 53-Q12
   Partnerships, 39-Q7

Purchase price allocations, 47-Q1

Qualified appraiser, 78-Q4

Qualifying contributions, 79-Q1

Quick ratio, 63-Q12

Rate of return
   Expected, 23-Q1
   Nominal, 23-Q3, 24-Q4
   Real, 23-Q3, 24-Q4

Ratio analysis
   Activity ratios, 59-Q2, 61-Q7
   Leverage ratios, 60-Q3, 61-Q8
   Liquidity ratios, 60-Q4

Real estate
   Appraisal certification, 47-Q3
   Compared with real property, 48-Q5
   Compared with business valuation
      methods, 48-Q10

Real property, 48-Q5

Real rate of return, 23-Q3, 24-Q4

Reasonable compensation disputes,
      49-Q3

Reconciliation, *see* value reconciliation

Regional economic data, 65-Q4, 65-Q6,
      73-Q14

Replacement cost, 16-Q5

Report, *see* valuation report

Residual value, *see* terminal value

Restricted stock studies, 52-Q6, 53-Q8

Return on investment, 62-Q10

Revenue Rulings (RRs)
   Generally, 4-Q9, 56-Q3
   59-60, 3-Q2, 39-Q6, 77-Q2, 78-Q5
   68-609, 3-Q2, 53-Q8
   66-49, 78-Q4
   77-287, 3-Q2, 53-Q8
   83-120, 3-Q2, 53-Q8
   93-12, 4-Q3, 53-Q8

Risk
   Business risk, 16-Q3
   Cost of capital, 23-Q3
   Default risk, 26-Q15
   Estimation, 27-Q21
   Financial risk, 16-Q3
   Horizon risk, 26-Q15
   Interest rate risk, 26-Q15
   Investment risk, 16-Q3
   Systematic risk, 15-Q1, 16-Q3,
      26-Q17, 28-Q32
   Time value of money, 24-Q4
   Unsystematic risk, 27-Q18

Risk Management Association (formerly
      Robert Morris Associates),
      64-Q1

Risk-free rate
   CAPM, 26-Q17
   Components, 26-Q15
   Cost of capital, 23-Q3
   Equity risk premium, 17-Q2, 27-Q24
   Intermediate-term, 27-Q19
   Long-term, 27-Q19
   Short-term, 27-Q19
   Time value of money, 24-Q4

Robert Morris Associates (now Risk
      Management Association),
      64-Q1

Rules of thumb, 47-Q2

S corporations, 79-Q1

Salvage (liquidation) method, 30-Q2

SEC Institutional Investor Study, 52-Q4,
      52-Q6, 74-Q15

Securities and Exchange Commission
(SEC)
10-K, 40-Q12
10-Q, 40-Q13
Disclosures, 39-Q9
Partnerships, 39-Q7
Special events report, 40-Q14
Service firms
Asset values, 55-Q2
Excess earnings method, 50-Q12
Inventory, 48-Q4
Shareholder disputes, *see* dissenting
stockholder actions and/or
minority oppression actions
SIC code, 39-Q10, 40-Q15
Silber Study, 52-Q6
Single-stage DCF model, 29-Q39
Site visits, 67-Q1, 67-Q2, 67-Q3,
68-Q5, 68-Q6
Size of block, 52-Q3
Size premium (small stock premium)
CAPM, 28-Q25
Equity risk premium, 26-Q16
Expanded CAPM, 27-Q18
Standard & Poor's (S&P)
500 Index (S&P 500), 17-Q2
Standard & Poor's Industry Surveys,
73-Q8
Standard deviation, 60-Q5
Standard of value
Generally, 15-Q2
Bankruptcy, 83-Q5
Buy-sell agreements, 83-Q6
Dissenting stockholder actions, 21-Q2
ESOPs, 21-Q1, 80-Q5
Fair market value, 8-Q2, 9-Q3,
16-Q4, 21-Q1, 21-Q2, 22-Q6,
24-Q5, 42-Q, 3, 77-Q1, 80-Q5,
83-Q4, 83-Q5, 83-Q6, 85-Q1,
86-Q5
Fair value, 8-Q2, 9-Q3, 10-Q7,
16-Q4, 21-Q2, 24-Q5, 77-Q1,
83-Q4, 83-Q5, 83-Q6, 85-Q1

Intrinsic value, 9-Q3, 16-Q4, 24-Q5,
77-Q1, 83-Q4, 83-Q5, 85-Q1
Investment value, 8-Q2, 9-Q3, 16-Q4,
24-Q5, 77-Q1, 83-Q4, 83-Q5,
83-Q6
Marital dissolution, 8-Q2, 22-Q3,
22-Q6, 85-Q1, 86-Q5
Minority oppression actions, 9-Q3,
83-Q4
Synergistic value, 51-Q1
Tax-related valuations, 21-Q1, 77-Q1
Transaction value, 9-Q4, 39-Q5
Standard Research Consultants Study,
52-Q4
State court system, 12-Q7
Statement of contingent and limiting
conditions, 10-Q10
Statement of Financial Accounting
Standard (SFAS) 142, 10-Q7
Statistical Abstract of the United States,
65-Q5
*Stocks, Bonds, Bills and Inflation
Yearbook*, 71-Q1
Subpoenas, 12-Q6
Subsequent events, 67-Q4
Subsidiary, cost of capital, 24-Q6
Summonses, 12-Q6
Survey of Buying Power, 65-Q5, 65-Q6
Survey of Current Business, 64-Q2,
65-Q6
Synergistic value, 51-Q1
Systematic risk, 15-Q1, 16-Q3, 26-Q17,
28-Q32

Tangible assets, 50-Q6
Tax Court, *see* U.S. Tax Court
Tax rate, 18-Q4, 25-Q9, 26-Q14
Tax return data, 64-Q2, 65-Q3, 66-Q8,
65-Q3
Tax-free rollover, 80-Q3, 80-Q9
Tax-related valuations
Buy-sell agreements, 45-Q3, 78-Q6

Tax-related valuations (*cont.*)
  Charitable contributions, 78-Q4, 78-Q8
  Discount for trapped-in capital gains, 48-Q7, 52-Q5
  Excess earnings method, 49-Q3
  Key person discount, 53-Q10
  Standard of value, 21-Q1, 77-Q1
Technical Advice Memorandums (TAMs), 4-Q8
Terminal value
  Generally, 18-Q4, 31-Q4
  Discrete projection period, 31-Q8
  Estimation, 30-Q2, 37-Q16, 37-Q17
Testimony, *see* expert witnesses
Time value of money, 24-Q4
Times interest earned, 59-Q2, 60-Q3, 60-Q4, 63-Q13
Transaction value, 9-Q4, 39-Q5
Trapped-in capital gains discount, *see* discount for trapped-in capital gains
Two-stage model
  Gordon Growth Model, 36-Q12
  Terminal value, 35-Q5

Uniform Standards of Professional Appraisal Practice (USPAP), 9-Q5, 48-Q8
Unlevered beta, 27-Q20, 29-Q38
Unsystematic risk, 27-Q18
U.S. Industry and Trade Outlook, 74-Q17
U.S. Tax Court
  Discount for trapped-in capital gains, 48-Q7, 52, Q5, 6-Q3
  Judgeships, 4-Q4
  Key person discount, 53-Q10
  Purpose, 12-Q8

Valuation Advisors' Lack of Marketability Discount Study™, 53-Q7

Valuation approach, 15-Q2, 22-Q8, 22-Q9, 22-Q10, 47-Q2, 55, Q1, 84-Q9, 84-Q10
Valuation date
  Dissenting stockholder suits, 8-Q1
  Engagement letter, 10-Q13
  Marital dissolutions, 86-Q6
  Relationship to period, 18-Q3
  Subsequent events, 67-Q4
Valuation engagement, fraud investigation, 10-Q11
Valuation methods, 83-Q3
Valuation multiples
  BIZCOMPS®, 42-Q6
  Coefficient of variation, 39-Q4, 56-Q5
  IBA Market Database, 42-Q5
  Invested capital, 38-Q1
  Mathematical weighting, 39-Q4
  Mergerstat/Shannon Pratt's Control Premium Study™, 43-Q8
  Pratt's Stats™, 43-Q7
  Public companies, 41-Q1
  Relationship with capitalization rate, 16-Q6
  Selection and weighting, 39-Q4, 56-Q5
  Subjective weighting, 39-Q4
Valuation procedure, 15-Q2, 84-Q10
Valuation purpose/use, 4-Q10, 10-Q13
Valuation report
  Elements of, 9-Q6
  Experts' written reports under FRCP, 11-Q1
  Statement of contingent and limiting conditions, 10-Q10
  Subsequent events, 67-Q4
Valuation Examiner, The (journal), 6-Q6
Valuation Strategies (journal), 6-Q6
Value Line Investment Survey, 72-Q6
Value reconciliation
  Asset values, 55-Q2
  Delaware Block Method, 56-Q4
  Weighting of approaches, 55-Q1, 84-Q10